To
(The Best Land Lady to live)
Thank you so much for all
of your support over these
years. It has been nothing
but a pleasure. Much Love

Danielle Rose

Does Your Face Look Like the Sun?

Donaylle Nicole

WestBow Press
A DIVISION OF THOMAS NELSON
& ZONDERVAN

Copyright © 2015 Donaylle Nicole.

All rights reserved. No part of this book may be used or reproduced by any means, graphic, electronic, or mechanical, including photocopying, recording, taping or by any information storage retrieval system without the written permission of the author except in the case of brief quotations embodied in critical articles and reviews.

Scripture taken from the King James Version of the Bible.

The information, ideas, and suggestions in this book are not intended as a substitute for professional medical advice. Before following any suggestions contained in this book, you should consult your personal physician. Neither the author nor the publisher shall be liable or responsible for any loss or damage allegedly arising as a consequence of your use or application of any information or suggestions in this book.

WestBow Press books may be ordered through booksellers or by contacting:

WestBow Press
A Division of Thomas Nelson & Zondervan
1663 Liberty Drive
Bloomington, IN 47403
www.westbowpress.com
1 (866) 928-1240

Because of the dynamic nature of the Internet, any web addresses or links contained in this book may have changed since publication and may no longer be valid. The views expressed in this work are solely those of the author and do not necessarily reflect the views of the publisher, and the publisher hereby disclaims any responsibility for them.

Any people depicted in stock imagery provided by Thinkstock are models, and such images are being used for illustrative purposes only.
Certain stock imagery © Thinkstock.

Craig Watson - Author photo

ISBN: 978-1-5127-1737-2 (sc)
ISBN: 978-1-5127-1738-9 (hc)
ISBN: 978-1-5127-1736-5 (e)

Library of Congress Control Number: 2015917906

Print information available on the last page.

WestBow Press rev. date: 12/02/2015

CONTENTS

Chapter 1	Does Your Face Look like the Sun?	1
Chapter 2	Feed Your Face	4
Chapter 3	From the Neck Down	15
Chapter 4	Get Your Mind Right	27
Chapter 5	Get Out of the Way!	39
Chapter 6	The Paradigm Shift	43
Chapter 7	Your Relationship with You	47
Chapter 8	How Well Are We Nourished?	57
Chapter 9	What Is a Soul Mate?	60
Chapter 10	Inspiration	63
Chapter 11	Do You Love Being Sick?	69
Chapter 12	Water Works	89
Chapter 13	Lavish Love	95
Chapter 14	Delightful, Delicate Details	100
Chapter 15	Quotes to Make Your Face Look like the Sun	103
Chapter 16	Who Are You, Anyway?	107
Chapter 17	Outside In Works Too	116
Chapter 18	Move It or Lose It!	123
Chapter 19	Vibrant Living	129
Chapter 20	Attitude of Gratitude	135

Chapter 1
Does Your Face Look like the Sun?

I received the most extraordinary compliment at an omelet bar one beautiful, sunny morning. Each morning during my vacation in Jamaica, I appreciated the chefs at the omelet station in the breakfast room. Maybe it was the fact that an abundance of warm sunlight filled the room. Maybe it was how the Caribbean air made my skin feel. Maybe it was being on an island so rich with beauty and simplicity and plenty to delight each of my senses. Maybe it was the fact that someone else cleaned up after me and prepared meals for me, with great flair and great care, or that I was on vacation with family and friends who enriched and nourished me in body, mind, and spirit. In any case, my appreciation on this particular vacation reached new altitudes when the omelet chef looked at me and said, "May I make an omelet for you, lady?" The moment I realized that this kind gentleman was speaking to me, I replied, "Yes, that would be lovely. Thank you."

He then asked if I knew why he wanted to prepare the omelet for me. Of course, I was curious because I had not approached his station; rather, he had called out to me. He said, "I have been watching you come in here morning after morning, and it is a joy when you come in because your face looks like the sun." My face often sends messages I don't realize I'm sending. It has often gotten me into hot water, as a matter of fact. My face and I are still trying to get on the same page.

At first, I wasn't sure how to feel about his remark. Yes, I realize the sun is warm and bright and glowing, but all I could think was that I somehow reminded him of a big, round, yellow ball that sets things on fire. Of course, I am exaggerating, but I really wasn't sure what he meant by it. Then I stopped to consider his expression. He was warm, friendly, sincere, and happy. Why would he suddenly say something rude? He wouldn't.

I received that comment several years ago, yet it has stayed with me. The more I think about it, the happier it makes me. Over time, it has come to be one of the greatest compliments of my adult life.

I absolutely adore the sun. I won't even wear sunscreen so I can absorb more sunlight into my skin. We need vitamin D, for heaven's sake. Besides, have you ever taken the time to actually read the ingredients in sunscreen? We should be far more scared to smear that on our skin than to let the sun's rays touch us. How else are we going to get our vitamin D levels to where they should be?

The sun has *so* many delicious benefits. Consider all the people with seasonal affective disorder. They are experiencing a deficiency in sunlight. Think of how crabbiness decreases on a sunny vacation or even just on a sunny day.

People often refer to November and February as the months during which they experience depression and anxiety. What do they do? They go to a tanning bed or book the quickest flight they can find to wherever the sun is shining brightly.

The sun represents so much that is positive and wonderful. Even perspiring more is a good thing because it detoxifies our bodies. How bad can that be? Caucasian people may not be as concerned with uneven skin tone, but for darker-skinned people, the chance to even out the various shades of brown is exciting. For those with naturally curly hair, the humidity in Caribbean air is a blessing. Never will those curls have better bounce. When the sunshine combines with humidity, you also experience more glow to your complexion. The air feels like heat combined with essential oils and lotions that saturate your skin. You need nothing more than to simply walk outside and appreciate it.

My vacation in Jamaica was pure delight, and it didn't hurt at all that we had a wonderful butler waiting on us hand and foot. Sunlight, anyone?

Chapter 2
Feed Your Face

After reflecting at length on how the face could look like the sun, I was inspired to create a series of classes around the topic. In running a hair salon, I get to speak to people all day long, especially women. They are more open to sharing concerns in a salon than they might be in a different arena because a hair salon is often considered a safe haven. People will share feelings and challenges about anything from how they look to how they feel to details about relationships, family, and traumas.

The Midwest really got hit hard with a snowstorm last winter, so creating something to uplift people sounded like a good idea. I came up with a four-part series with the theme, "Does Your Face Look like the Sun?" If I had not had such a crazy title, who would have opened the e-mail or read the blog post about it? The classes supported that theme in various ways.

The first class was called "Feed Your Face!" and was a literal interpretation of the theme. A chef prepared superfoods for all who attended. I wanted participants to know that we can give a glow to our skin by eating food prepared in a way that delights the palate.

Most people don't think about how food affects our skin, but it has a huge impact. Skin is the largest organ of the body, and it must not be ignored. These classes taught people how food can be used to reduce inflammation, lines, and wrinkles and to rebuild and support collagen and elasticity in order to fight premature aging. How we age can be greatly affected by the choices we make about what we put into our mouths. We must realize that food is the most powerful drug in existence. Do we ever consider the fact that no cell in the human body is made from a drug? So why do people most often solve health problems as if they suffer from some medicinal deficiency? If I have a headache, it is not because I have a Tylenol deficiency!

When was the last time you took a nice, long look at your freshly cleaned face to see what you could do to improve its appearance from the inside out? Look closely at the texture, pore size, color, and level of congestion in the skin. In this information age, there is no reason we can't learn what will nourish us and literally change the way we look. Pay attention to your reflection to better know what you should feed your face.

Superfoods and Recipes

Eggs	Strawberries
Tomato sauce	Lentils
Dried plums (prunes)	Bran flakes
Walnuts	Kiwi
Brussels sprouts	Black beans
Acai juice	Sunflower seeds
Apples	Sardines
Salmon	Asparagus
Avocados	Bananas
Spinach	Broccoli sprouts
Canned pumpkin	Baked potatoes
Cauliflower	Sweet potatoes
Scallops	Flaxseed
Collard greens	Greek yogurt
Olives	Blueberries
Brown rice	Oranges
Edamame	Watercress

Superfood Smoothie*

Servings: 1

Ingredients:
3 celery stalks
1 large cucumber
1 small beet
1 tablespoon of fresh ginger
½ Fuji apple (or any apple you like)
1 cup coconut water

Instructions:
Place ingredients in a high-powered juicer and juice. Drink immediately.

*Can be used as a lunch replacement.

Long-Life Cocktail*

Servings: 1

Ingredients:
1 apple
1 bunch of kale
½ lemon
2 celery stalks

Instructions:
Place ingredients in a high-powered juicer and juice. Drink immediately.

*Can be used as a breakfast replacement.

Grilled Wild Salmon with Avocado Salsa
Servings: 4

Ingredients:
2 pounds salmon fillets

Seasoning mix:
1 teaspoon salt
1 teaspoon coriander, ground
1 teaspoon cumin, ground
1 teaspoon paprika
1 teaspoon onion powder
1 teaspoon black pepper
4 tablespoons olive oil

Instructions:
- Preheat grill.
- Mix salt, coriander, cumin, paprika, onion, and black pepper to make seasoning mix. Rub salmon fillets with olive oil and seasoning mix. Let marinate in refrigerator for 30 minutes.
- Grill salmon to desired doneness.

Avocado Salsa*
Ingredients:
1 avocado, peeled, seeded, and sliced
1 small red onion, sliced
3 hot peppers, mild
juice of 2 limes
3 tablespoons olive oil
2 teaspoons cilantro, finely chopped
salt to taste
capers (optional)
Latin-style rice or plantain chips

Instructions:
Combine all ingredients except chips and stir. Chill. Serve salmon topped with avocado salsa and chips on the side.

Suggested side dish: wild or brown rice

Healthy Blueberry Breakfast Cookies

Servings: 12 cookies

Ingredients:
1 ½ cup oats
1 cup unsweetened coconut flakes
1 tablespoon golden flaxseed meal
½ teaspoon salt
¾ cup pecans, coarsely chopped
½ cup dried blueberries
3 ripe bananas, mashed
¼ cup coconut oil, melted
1 tablespoon agave nectar
1 teaspoon vanilla extract

Instructions:
- Preheat oven to 350 degrees.
- In a large bowl, combine oats, coconut flakes, flaxseed meal, salt, pecans, and blueberries.
- Stir in bananas, coconut oil, agave nectar, and vanilla extract until well combined.
- Spray cookie sheet with cooking spray. Take a generous spoonful of mixture and form it into a ball. Place on cookie sheet and softly press down with palm of hand. Repeat until mixture is completely used.
- Bake at 350 degrees for 25 minutes or to desired doneness.
- Cool and enjoy!

Skinny Cookies*
Servings: 12 cookies

Ingredients:
2 medium ripe bananas, mashed
1 cup quick oats, uncooked
¼ cup walnuts, crushed

Instructions:
- Preheat oven to 350 degrees. Spray cookie sheet with cooking spray.
- Combine bananas and oats in a bowl and stir. Add walnuts and mix in.
- Scoop one tablespoon of dough onto cookie sheet. Repeat until mixture is gone.
- Bake 15 minutes.

*Best when served immediately.

Low-Fat Chocolate Breakfast Cookie
Servings: 12 Cookies

Ingredients:
2 medium ripe bananas, mashed
1 cup quick oats, uncooked
¼ cup semi-sweet chocolate chips

Instructions:
- Preheat oven to 350 degrees. Spray a nonstick cookie sheet with cooking spray.
- Combine the mashed bananas and oats in a bowl.
- Fold in the chocolate chips.

- Place a tablespoon of mixture into hands. Form into a ball and then place on cookie sheet, softly pressing down with palm. Repeat until mixture is gone.
- Bake 15 minutes.

Cookie Ingredient Substitutes
Substitute the traditional ingredients for cookies with these healthier options.

Ingredients:

coconut oil
whole wheat flour
oats
toasted almonds
ripe mashed bananas

dried blueberries
flaxseed, ground
dark chocolate chips
Chia seeds

Detox Water*
Ingredients:
6 cups filtered water
1 tablespoon grated ginger
1 cucumber, sliced
1 lemon, sliced
1/3 cup mint leaves

Instructions:
Place all ingredients into a water infuser and let infuse overnight. Drink throughout the next day.

*Flattens abs and detoxifies the system.

Collard and Kale Salad with Lemon Garlic Dressing

Servings: 4

Ingredients:
½ cup olive oil
juice of 2 lemons
1 clove of garlic, minced
2 teaspoons Dijon mustard
2 teaspoons kosher salt
1 tablespoon raw honey
1 tablespoon chopped basil
1 bunch of collard greens, finely chopped
1 bunch of kale, finely chopped
2 avocados, cut into ½-inch cubes
4 carrots, peeled and grated
1 pint of cherry tomatoes, halved
½ red onion, finely chopped
¼ cup Parmesan cheese, shredded
walnuts (optional)
bacon (optional)

Instructions:
- Whisk together olive oil, honey, lemon juice, garlic, Dijon mustard, and salt. Refrigerate dressing for 1 hour.
- In a large bowl, combine remaining ingredients. Toss gently with dressing until all ingredients are covered.

Fruit Salad
Servings: 8

Ingredients:
2 apricots
1 pomegranate
2 peaches
1 pineapple
3 apples
1 ½ cup blueberries
2 tablespoons organic raw honey
1 cup walnuts
1 teaspoon vanilla extract
½ teaspoon cinnamon
¼ teaspoon nutmeg

Instructions:
Toss all ingredients in a large bowl.

Salmon Lettuce Wraps
Servings: 8

Ingredients:
4 (12-ounce) wild salmon fillets
2 teaspoons sesame oil
½ teaspoon five-spice powder*
¼ teaspoon salt
¼ cup creamy peanut butter
¼ cup hoisin sauce
1 tablespoon lime juice
1 tablespoon soy sauce
1 teaspoon fresh grated ginger
1 ½ tablespoon hot red chili paste

¼ cup apple cider vinegar
½ cup carrots, julienned
½ cup peanuts, dry roasted
½ cup cilantro leaves, fresh chopped
¼ cup chopped red onion
½ cup sweet red peppers, julienned
½ cup snow peas, julienned
8 Bibb or iceberg lettuce leaves, trimmed to form cup shape

*Five- spice powder may include 1 ½ tablespoon star anise, 2 ½ teaspoons fennel seeds, 1 ½ teaspoons cassia (or cinnamon), ½ teaspoon szechwan pepper, ½ teaspoon cloves

Instructions:
- Preheat broiler. Spray pan with cooking spray.
- Place salmon on pan, skin facing down. Broil for 5 minutes.
- Preheat oven to 375 degrees. Spread sesame oil over salmon and rub five-spice powder and salt on fish.
- Bake for 4 minutes or until fish is baked through.
- Remove skin and shred fish into large chunks.
- Place peanut butter, hoisin sauce, lime juice, soy sauce, ginger, and chili paste into food processor and pulse until smooth. Pour in vinegar into mixture and pulse until mixture forms into a sauce consistency.
- In a medium bowl, combine carrots, peanuts, cilantro, onion, peppers, peas, peanut butter sauce (to your liking), and salmon. Mix together.
- Serve mixture in large lettuce leaves and enjoy!

Chapter 3
From the Neck Down

Obviously, we must care about more than just our faces. It's only reasonable that we also consider how we're doing from the neck down. How do we feel overall? Do we have a lot of pep in our step, or are we dragging? When we wake up in the morning, is it fairly easy to get going? When our friends describe us, what words do they use? Do we hear things like *happy, energetic*, and *healthy*?

When I was planning the event "From the Neck Down," I decided to research lands where people live the longest and have the greatest quality of life in their later years. Consistently, Japan and the Mediterranean kept surfacing.

Looking into what the people there do differently from those in the Western parts of the world seemed like a great way to create more wellness. Japan, in particular, has more people who live to be one hundred years old than anywhere else on this planet. It's not just that they live to be that old but that they are truly living life.

In this part of the world (the United States), we may have plenty of people who make it to one hundred years old, but what quality of life are they living? For the most part, isn't it a life of illness, pain medication, assisted-living facilities, nursing homes, rocking chairs, and loneliness?

Did you know that there are parts of the world where things like cancer, diabetes, heart disease, and stroke are next to nonexistent? Can you guess why? People in those parts of the world are much more savvy about a holistic approach to their well-being. It is not strange to those from Eastern countries to use nutrition, vitamins and supplements, essential oils, herbs, teas, juicing, and massage to treat illness.

They are more proactive, rather than reactive, about health care. The common philosophy on health in this country is often to wait until we get sick before we pay any attention to our bodies and how we treat them.

It is very common in this society to place little emphasis on the quality of food that goes into our mouths. We rarely make the connection between what type of fuel we put into our tanks and how our bodies perform. Much more care is taken about the kind of gas and oil that goes into our vehicles than the type and amount of fuel we put inside our own bodies.

This is not the case in other parts of the world. From a young age, children are taught where their food comes from, what it means to eat in season, and what is healthy and what is not. I saw a television show on which American children were being interviewed about food. A well-known chef from England was asking kids where they thought different foods came from. I was stunned. These kids did not know that milk came from cows, eggs came from chickens, or which meat came from which animal. For example, they didn't know that hamburger was beef and that beef comes from cows. The most shocking statement of all came from one little boy who thought that honey came from bears!

Apparently, our approach to taking care of ourselves from the neck down needs more attention. We can learn much from the Mediterranean countries, as well as Japanese culture. We should take a closer look at their diet, their lifestyle, and their general approach to well-being.

We should be interested in why the elderly in Japan are out fishing, gardening, shopping, and moving about in life, just like everybody else. They're not chained to chairs, sick, in pain, or living in nursing homes with bedpans. They have vigor and vitality that are often greater than those of a fifty- or sixty-year-old in this country.

My dad had to have kidney surgery a couple of years ago to have some cancerous tumors removed. Naturally, since we wanted him to receive the greatest care possible, we encouraged him to go to a world-renowned hospital, and he chose to take that advice.

When my family arrived at the hospital at five o'clock in the morning to be there for the surgery, which was to begin two hours later. The scene was downright spooky. As we entered the surgical area of the hospital, we realized just how out of control things really were. It was an area reserved only for cancer surgeries, and our dad was one of about one hundred patients getting prepped for a seven o'clock cancer surgery. The patients about to go under the knife were moving through the place like cattle, all lined up in a row. Our dad was really only a number.

Later, my brother-in-law approached a nurse and asked about the number of pop machines and junk food vending machines in the cancer department. The nurse looked at him like he was stupid and said, "What do pop and snacks have to do with cancer?" Scary! Even those in the medical profession know very little about how much food affects our health and our vitality. What a shame. People put so much faith, trust, and hope in their physicians. They do what they are told, they fill those prescriptions, they pop those pills, and they even undergo surgery.

What if it all could have been prevented by being proactive rather than reactive? What if people really applied the rule, "An apple a day will keep the doctor away"? What if we did drink our eight glasses of water a day? Most people are walking around chronically dehydrated and don't even realize it.

My sister spent a couple of weeks in Italy eating more pasta, gelato, bread, and cheese and drinking more wine than ever before. Surely she gained a bunch of weight during her stay, right? Wrong! She and my brother-in-law both lost weight and had never felt lighter and more fit and healthy.

The evening meal in Italy can be served as late as nine o'clock and go on until eleven o'clock. Dining for the evening meal is quite the event, often lasting two to three hours. Course after course is brought to the table, paired with wines to enhance the food. So how did my sister and brother-in-law get away with that? How was it that they didn't see obese people everywhere?

There were several things going on in Italy that are different from how we do things in the United States. For starters, lots of fresh vegetables were incorporated into each meal. Another consideration is the food itself. It was locally grown, eaten in season, prepared from scratch, and not genetically modified. Can you believe it? Some people in this world don't eat cloned food. How about that?

Another reason that my sister and her husband gained no weight was the amount of movement they got during any given day. My sister is a fitness fanatic and works out strenuously five or six times per week. In Italy, it would have been unnecessary for her to work out at a gym because she walked everywhere and always took the stairs. She could just throw in some exercises for upper body strength and some stretching, and she was all set.

When we complete a big meal with dessert and wine in the States, the next stop is typically the couch. It is not our natural inclination to eat a meal slowly, really savoring the flavors so that we are content with a much smaller portion. Most of us don't get right up and head out for a long walk after dinner. But in Italy, since my sister and her husband walked everywhere, calories didn't get a chance to stick to them. They could burn everything off before retiring for the day. Why not try that one on for size to see if you notice a difference in how you feel? After all, if we don't move it, we will lose it, right?

In Japan, meat consumption is very low, while vegetables, fish, and seaweed are eaten in abundance. Meat is thought of as something you use to add flavor or to spice up a dish. There, you won't walk by anybody's dinner table and see a huge T-bone steak with a loaded baked potato full of bacon and cheese, a hunk of yeasty bread, and a dinner salad made with iceberg lettuce topped with ranch, bacon bits, cheese, and croutons.

Anyone want to rethink what to order the next time we dine out? What about incorporating some Lebanese food if seaweed and fish don't excite you? Lebanese food offers tremendous flavor, variety, visual interest, and health. I love it, actually! Eating foods from other lands is a great way to expand culturally, in addition to learning healthy tips. What a great education it offers us. Try the following recipes on for size.

"Let food be thy medicine and let medicine be thy food." —Hippocrates

Eye-Opener Juice

Servings: 2

Ingredients:
2 green apples, seeds removed
1 small cucumber
1 small beet root
¼ lemon, seeds removed
½- inch slice of ginger

Instructions:
Place ingredients into juicer and juice.

Green Detox Juice

Servings: 2

Ingredients:
2 apples, seeds removed
1 celery stalk
1-inch slice of ginger
½ lemon, seeds removed
½ bunch of spinach
1 handful watercress

Instructions:
Place ingredients into juicer and juice. If you prefer more of a smoothie texture, add ice and use blender instead of juicer.

Carrot-Pineapple Smoothie
Servings: 2

Ingredients:
¾ cup fresh pineapple, chopped
½ cup ice
1/3 cup fresh orange juice
¼ cup carrots, chopped
½ banana

Instructions:
Place all ingredients in blender and blend until smooth and frothy.

Kale Quinoa Superfood Salad
Servings: 4

Ingredients:
1 cup quinoa, cooked
1 cup blueberries
½ cup almonds
1 carrot, grated
1 bunch kale
1 clove garlic
1 teaspoon ginger
1 cup grape or cherry tomatoes
1 sheet seaweed, toasted

Dressing
1/8 cup balsamic vinegar
1 tablespoon soy sauce, low sodium
1 tablespoon honey

¼ cup extra-virgin olive oil
½ teaspoon sesame oil
1 tablespoon water

Instructions:
- Cook quinoa according to package directions and let cool.
- Meanwhile, blend dressing ingredients in blender and pulse until smooth.
- In a large mixing bowl, combine blueberries, almonds, carrot, kale, quinoa, garlic, ginger, and tomatoes and stir together. Add dressing to your liking.
- Top with sliced seaweed (nori) if desired and serve.

Roasted Garlic Baba Ghanoush
Servings: 4

Ingredients:
2 tablespoons olive oil
2 eggplants, medium
1 small head garlic
3 tablespoons lemon juice
2 tablespoons tahini
½ tablespoon salt

Instructions:
- Preheat oven to 400 degrees.
- Cut the top off the head of garlic. Place on a sheet of foil and drizzle with olive oil. Wrap tightly in foil and place on a rimmed baking sheet with the eggplants.
- Roast the veggies for 45 minutes or until the eggplants collapse and the garlic is soft throughout.

- Cut the eggplants in half lengthwise and place in a colander to cool and drain. Open the garlic packet to cool.
- Peel the eggplants, and squeeze the flesh from the garlic head. Place all ingredients in the food processor and pulse to desired consistency.
- Serve with pita bread or raw veggies for a healthier choice

Falafel

Servings: 4

Ingredients:
coconut oil
1 can of chickpeas, drained
1 large onion, chopped
2 cloves of garlic, chopped
3 tablespoons fresh parsley, chopped
1 teaspoon coriander
1 teaspoon cumin
salt (to taste)
pepper (to taste)
2 tablespoons flour (or coconut flour)

Instructions:
- Preheat oven to 375 degrees. Coat baking sheet with coconut oil.
- Place chickpeas, onion, garlic, parsley, flour, coriander, cumin, and salt and pepper into a food processor. Blend until there is a paste consistency.
- Form mixture into balls the size of a ping-pong ball and place on cooking sheet. Slightly flatten using palm of hand. (Add more flour if mixture is not sticking together.)
- Place sheet in oven and cook for 8 minutes or until slightly brown on bottom.
- Serve with tahini or in a whole-wheat pita bread with lettuce, tomatoes, and onion.

Chicken Shawarma

Servings: 4

Chicken
Ingredients:
2 tablespoons lemon juice
1 teaspoon curry powder
2 teaspoons olive oil
¾ teaspoon salt
½ teaspoon ground cumin
3 garlic cloves, minced
1 pound boneless, skinless chicken breast, cut into strips

Sauce
Ingredients:
½ cup Greek yogurt
2 tablespoons tahini
2 teaspoons lemon juice
¼ teaspoon salt
1 garlic clove, minced

You will also need:
Whole wheat pitas
1 cup chopped romaine lettuce
1 medium tomato, sliced

Instructions:
- Preheat grill to medium-high heat.
- In a medium bowl, combine first six ingredients. Add chicken to bowl and evenly coat each piece with mixture. Let sit for 20 minutes.
- In a separate bowl, combine yogurt, tahini, lemon juice, salt, and garlic. Whisk together and set aside.
- Thread 2 chicken strips onto a skewer. Place on grill (coated with cooking spray); grill each side for 4 minutes or until done.

- Place pitas on grill rack. Grill one minute on each side or until slightly toasted.
- Top pita with chicken, lettuce, and tomato. Drizzle sauce on top and serve.

Alternative: Serve with rice and grilled veggies.

Chapter 4
Get Your Mind Right

The mind–body connection has always intrigued me. In my early twenties, I began to suffer from debilitating back pain. It felt like someone was wrapping his arms around my waist from behind to pull me to the ground. In fact, at times, the pain was so severe that I could not get up off the ground. Sometimes I just lay there crying, feeling helpless and hopeless.

Here is what really made it strange—I had never suffered any injuries. I had not pulled anything, strained anything, fallen down, run into anything, or lifted anything too heavy. One day, it just started, and the suffering lasted for two whole years.

I tried every type of treatment during that time. Chiropractors did their thing, massage therapists of every kind tried to help me out, an acupuncturist put needles in my body, and reflexologists worked on my feet. I ingested anti-inflammatory pills, along with muscle relaxers, all to no avail. Relief finally came when my husband told me about a type of treatment that we had never heard of before. It was during this alternative health treatment that I learned about the power of our minds over how the body performs.

We've all heard the phrase, "Stress kills," but never could I have imagined how true that is. Literally, I could not get up off of the floor because of stress. Why do you think we have expressions like "pain in the neck"? Even being around certain people can cause so much anxiety that our muscles tense up and we end up with headaches and tension knots in our necks, backs, and shoulders. People who hate their jobs often suffer from migraine headaches or digestion issues like irritable bowel syndrome or colitis.

What can be done? We can't always control whom we are around. We can't always control whether or not an employment situation is ideal. Yet there is something that we are always in control of. You guessed it! Our minds.

One of the greatest powers we can master is how to control our thinking. It takes practice because it is counterintuitive to be superfocused on the thoughts we are thinking. When I realized how impactful my thoughts were to the quality of my life, I decided it was well worth the effort to learn how to focus.

A great way to know whether our thoughts are serving us in a positive was is to pay attention to how we feel. Stop—really stop—and focus. Focus on your breathing. Is it deep, or is it shallow? Could you benefit from slowing down to take some deep breaths in a quiet place, to oxygenate your cells and take inventory of how your body feels? Maybe if we were more mindful of our breathing, we wouldn't need so many antianxiety pills.

Try this exercise for five minutes. Set a timer. Breathe deeply with your eyes closed, and take inventory of your body. After the five minutes, write down your observations.

Do you have any pain? Do you realize that most people have no idea how good their bodies are supposed to feel? Isn't it nuts? Sometimes I just listen to what people talk about. More often than not, people are talking about their aches, pains, discomforts, or some other complaint.

It is pretty sad that, at times, I feel embarrassed to admit how good I typically feel. Working circles around those half my age is my life. The whining and complaining that can be heard from kids as young as preteens about feeling pain is frightening! Kids should not be in pain, but then again, they shouldn't be stressed out, and we know they *are* stressed these days. Stressed minds lead to diseased bodies, or *dis-ease*. Get it? Being uneasy about too many things for too long leads to dis-ease in our bodies.

We must stop treating symptoms. This is no way to have a high-quality life experience. We've got to be proactive with ourselves instead of waiting around to fall apart and then treating our symptoms.

Furthermore, if thoughts really do become reality, shouldn't we put a bit more focus on taking care of ourselves mentally and emotionally? Have you ever met someone who is superhappy, positive, fit, and abundant but who is also sick all the time? Not likely! Conversely, doesn't it seem like people who are always sick, broke, and tired are "Debbie Downers"?

Pay attention to what people talk about; really take note of what types of people talk about what types of things. What are their energy levels? What kind of relationships are they in? What types of lifestyles are they living? Do they travel or participate in anything creative or artistic? Do they have a glow about them or any light to their spirit?

Keep in mind that we become like the people we spend the most time with. Really think about that. If you are not happy with your life, take a look at whom you spend the most time with. This influence is so powerful that it even affects our finances. Take this challenge. List the five people that you are closest to and estimate each friend's annual income. Divide the number by 5. You will be amazed at how closely this number will resemble your own income. Basically, if you are unhappy with your finances, you might want to take a look at these friends.

We cannot control the mind-sets of our friends, but we can certainly work harder to control our own. Once we have a better handle on ‾ing a healthier mind-set, it is amazing what naturally begins Suddenly, we enjoy more positive, nourishing, nurturing relationships that serve us in more positive ways. When you can control your thoughts, you have greater quality control over your entire life. When we learn to change our minds, we can literally change our lives.

We've all met people for whom things just always seem to work out. For some people, it seems that everything they touch turns to gold. Doors of opportunity open up to them every time they turn around. They have such wonderful lives, and they seem genuinely happy.

Sit and contemplate the people you have come across who are like that. Write their names on a piece of paper. Next to each person, write the qualities that you notice in them. When you have a decent number of people on your list, look to see what characteristics they all have in common. Pay attention to what they talk about and what their energy levels are like.

Have you ever heard of a self-fulfilling prophecy? This is a reason to talk about what we want rather than what we do not want. The mind responds more quickly and more powerfully when we speak in affirmative statements—for example, saying, "I am nicotine-free," rather than, "I don't smoke."

This is tricky at first because it is counterintuitive. Most people spend a lot of time talking about what they do not want rather than what they do want, and then they wonder why they are experiencing the very things they do not want. Another example would be describing the type of relationships we want to have. Too often people make statements like, "I hate when guys do this" or "I hate when guys are like that toward me." Guess what? They end up attracting the very qualities from a partner that they said they did not want.

Clearly, what we think about and what we talk about can have a huge impact on our lives. Therefore, you can assume that it will serve you well to learn to focus. We need to pay attention to what thoughts are going through our heads and what words are coming out of our mouths.

When you catch yourself having a negative thought, change it! When you want an indication of how you are doing with this, pay attention to how your body feels. If you feel great, you can assume you are succeeding in getting your mind right!

Exercise

Pay attention to how you feel.

Stop!
- Start with your breathing. Is it fast, slow, deep, shallow, or balanced?
- Work down to the neck and shoulders. Is there any tension? Are there knots or pains?
- How about your arms and legs? Do they feel heavy, light, strong, weak, sore, or tired?
- Are you tired right now? If so, why? Do you need a twenty-minute nap, or did you not sleep well last night? Did you eat too much heavy food?
- Are you thirsty?
- How does your heart feel? Is it beating normally, or is it racing?
- What is your flexibility like? If you bend down, can you touch the floor easily?
- What is your balance like? How long can you stand on one foot before you fall over?
- What about your gut? Is it bloated, crampy, or burning?
- When you look at your hands, feet, or ankles, do they appear swollen due to holding excess fluid?

Does Your Face Look Like the Sun?

Really pay attention. We do not have anything going on with our bodies that was not caused by something. Plug in and feel how you feel. Once we know how we feel physically, it will be easier to access how we are doing mentally and emotionally.

Exercise

List your five closest friends.
1.
2.
3.
4.
5.

Now estimate their incomes.
1.
2.
3.
4.
5.

Total: $ _____

Divide the total of their incomes by 5: $ _____

Compare with your income: $ _____

Exercise

List the ten happiest people you know, if you know ten. If not, list as many as possible.

1.
2.
3.
4.
5.
6.
7.
8.
9.
10.

List the qualities they possess as they relate to health, vitality, income, conversation style, and interests.

1.
2.
3.
4.
5.
6.
7.
8.
9.
10.

Does Your Face Look Like the Sun?

Now look to see what they all have in common.

1.
2.
3.
4.
5.
6.
7.
8.
9.
10.

Take note of how consistently positive, abundant people love and notice their mind-sets.

Exercise

List the ten most negative people you know.

1.
2.
3.
4.
5.
6.
7.
8.
9.
10.

List the qualities they possess as they relate to health, vitality, income, conversation style, and interests.

1.
2.
3.
4.
5.
6.
7.
8.
9.
10.

Now list the attributes that they all have in common:

1.
2.
3.
4.
5.
6.
7.
8.
9.
10.

Compare your list of happy people with your list of negative people. Now compile a list of your personal characteristics, health and energy levels, conversation style, income, and so on.

Look to see which group most resembles your personal mind-set. Be honest with yourself. Where you are is where you are. Once you know better, then you can do better.

Inspiring Brain Foods

- Vitamin E provides vitality.
- Spinach gives you brain power.
- Eggs improve memory and focus.
- Lean red meat helps with iron for improved mental function. Iron deficiency blocks oxygen flow, causing mental fatigue.
- Walnuts are rich in omega-3 fatty acids and high in antioxidants, which promote brain function.
- Yerba maté tea energizes the mind.
- Lentils are rich in foliates, a type of B vitamin that enhances brain power and improves brain performance and mood.
- Beets give a blast of genius to your brain and encourage blood flow to the brain.
- Oats, the brain's favorite source of glucose, power the brain all day.
- Sardines help with focus by boosting cells and neurotransmitters in the brain.
- Flax or flax oil boosts the cerebral cortex. This area of the brain registers touch and taste and repairs damage or stress to the brain and nerve tissue.

If you are wondering what became of my two-year back pain, it is long gone. After being a guinea pig for two years, allowing practitioner after practitioner to *practice* medicine on me, I tried natural health care. After one treatment involving the whole person and not simply bandaging symptoms, I was pain-free in three days. That experience changed my entire life. If we do not have our health, what do we have? Being sick most of the time is so limiting to the quality of life we can experience. Had I not gone through those two years of pain, I might never have learned how important it is to pay attention to how my body feels. Never again would I blow off a headache or ignore congestion or allergy symptoms. Asking why is how I choose to live. I refuse to accept that *dis-ease* comes from nothing and nowhere. How horrible would it be to have absolutely no control whatsoever regarding my quality of life!

It is such a relief to me to know that if I abuse my body in any way, it will not be kind to me. We reap what we sow. If I wake up exhausted, I can usually figure out pretty quickly why that is. People just do not typically want to be that accountable for how they feel. It creates so much peace of mind to learn more about how the body works and what we can do and not do to affect its ability to perform well. Learning the mind–body connection is a huge step to "getting your mind right!"

Chapter 5
Get Out of the Way!

Who am I telling to get out of the way? Actually, it is no one other than the man or woman in the mirror. We've all heard that said before. "Get out of your own way" is a fairly common expression. The things that must get out of the way in order for us to thrive are any limiting beliefs we hold.

A belief is nothing more than a thought that we keep thinking. Remember the story of the woman learning how to cook a pot roast? As the story goes, her mother taught her that she must cut the ends off before placing it in the roasting pot, as her mother had taught her. Many generations believed that this was the secret to a truly moist, delicious pot roast. Finally, she decided to do some digging. She eventually found a member of the family who was old enough to explain the origins of this belief.

The elderly family member laughed at the only one who was inquisitive enough to ask. She told her that cutting the ends was not done for taste, texture, or even tenderness but because, when she had started cooking herself, beef roast was too large for her small pot and that was the only way to make it fit!

How about that! Person after person had bought into that limiting belief on the correct way to make a pot roast without ever investigating why they believed it. Sadly, human nature causes us to do that very thing with issues and topics that are much weightier. We don't stop to ask ourselves why we believe what we believe. We don't ask, "Where did that belief come from?" or "Is that person qualified to know the correct belief, anyway?"

It is scary! How do we know for sure that we are not going through life without reaching our full potential because our limiting beliefs are running the show? What would our lives look like if we challenged our current beliefs? What would we change? How would we look? How would we feel? With whom would we be friends? What career paths would we choose? What would we weigh? How much money would be in our savings accounts? How many children would we have? What kind of people would we be married to? What gifts and talents would we possess?

Exercise

Write down your current beliefs on these topics:

How do I look?
How do I feel?
Who are my friends?
Which career path did I choose?
What do I weigh?
How much is in my bank account?
How many children do I have?
What kind of person am I married to?
What gifts, talents, and abilities do I possess?
Where have I traveled?

Now consider this: If I got all limitations, fears, doubts, old thinking patterns, and attitudes out of my way, how would these answers change? How would my life look without limiting beliefs?

How do I look?
How do I feel?
Who are my friends?
Which career path did I choose?
What do I weigh?
How much is in my bank account?
How many children do I have?
What kind of man am I married to?

What gifts, talents, and abilities do I possess?

Where have I traveled?

After completing both lists, write a summary of how you feel about your discovery.

"The great opportunity is where you are." —John Burroughs

Chapter 6
The Paradigm Shift

This really is a very simple formula to creating more of what you want: you can never change your life until you change your thinking. Mind-set makes all the difference as to the quality and quantity of our life experience.

We've already questioned a few beliefs that we live our lives by, but those topics only scratched the surface. We can go much, much deeper with more profound topics. What are our beliefs about love, relationships, government, religion, genetically modified foods, animal cruelty, abortion, war, peace, and on and on?

After considering how you feel about things like that, I challenge you to question where those beliefs came from. Who taught you to believe what you believe? Who or what is your guidance system? Are your sources credible? Do your beliefs serve you in a really positive way?

When we step past accepting random opinions or popular beliefs, amazing things will begin to happen. So many lovely things will be allowed to flow because we haven't pinched off every beautiful experience, opportunity, and relationship due to negative, limiting thoughts and beliefs.

The only difference between a thought and a belief is the length of time spent dwelling on the topic. That is why it is so vital that we focus. Once we realize we are thinking a thought that does not serve us, we must be quick to change the thought so that it does not turn into a belief that can affect our mind-sets.

One example of a limiting belief is people's general attitude about money. Have you ever heard, "Money doesn't grow on trees," "There's no such thing as an easy buck," or "You have to spend money to make money"? What would happen if we had never bought into any of this? Have you ever stopped to really question whether these beliefs hold up? Here's an example. Let's say that every day, one of my children would ask me for money in various amounts. If my son asked me for five dollars and I gave it to him, did he have to spend any money to get it? I am pretty sure that qualifies as an "easy buck"—or an easy five bucks. For that child, it would be like money growing on trees.

Rarely will I speak in terms of lack. Now, I must tell you, this was a hard habit to break. It is very counterintuitive to speak abundance, to think abundant thoughts, and to stop worrying about not having enough. When we are lavish with our generosity, it makes us feel so good. When we hold on tightly to all that we have, it makes us feel miserable. We're focused on not-enough-ness and lack, which do not make us feel good. We feel good when things are flowing and moving rather than staying stuck in a rut. Flow always feels better. That is why we feel so good when we clear our closets of all the things we have not used in the last year and donate those items to a friend in need or give them to charity.

"Let go; let flow!" I heard that when we release things, we open the way for new things to flow into our experience. It is interesting to see how we are blessed when we are lavish with our full generosity. We don't have to participate in other attitudes and beliefs about money or anything else, for that matter.

Remember the economic crash that happened back around 2007 and 2008? I remember it very well because I was staying at an exquisite hotel in the center of Times Square in New York City, celebrating my fifteenth wedding anniversary. The thing that was constantly on the news was the economy.

"Oh, my goodness!" someone said. If I never heard that expression again, I decided, it would be too soon. There I was in Manhattan, SoHo, the Village, and Times Square, enjoying abundance all around me and seeing those around me doing the same, but all the media wanted to talk about was how bad this economic disaster was.

You want to know what I did? I stopped listening. You see, I decided that, for my family and my business, it would not serve me well to focus on not-enough-ness. We even told the hotel staff that they were not allowed to discuss the economy in any negative way because we were not going to be participating in the attitudes, thoughts, and behavior of those complaining about the economy. Rather than shop less, we shopped more. Rather than not offering donations to charity, we did more for charity. Rather than buy cheaper gifts, we bought nicer gifts.

It became my pleasure to spend money because I looked at it as a way of not making things worse. Contributing to fiscal flow, which is a must for economic health, made me feel really good. It made me feel abundant. Did it turn out to be only a feeling? Nope! In 2008, my business brought in more money than ever before, which means I made more money than I ever had. Really, it was supposed to be the worst year ever!

We were told to cut coupons, stop eating out, stop traveling, stop shopping, and stop going to the movies. It was hogwash for those who chose to ignore the whole stinking mess; we simply chose not to participate.

This can apply to so many things that do not positively affect us. Who cares what popular opinion is? If we don't use our brains, what is the point of having them? We don't have to follow the crowds who love to get in their own way. We can **get out of our own way!**

> "Wealth is the ability to fully experience life."
> —Henry David Thoreau

Chapter 7
Your Relationship with You

If you were to overhear someone describe your friendship with him or her, what might you hear? Would your friends say that they like you because you have a generous spirit? Would they say they like you because you have an attitude of gratitude? Would they say that they love coming to your home because you are hospitable? Are you known for not forgetting the things that matter to your friends, like their favorite colors, foods, or fragrances?

If someone were to ask you to describe your greatest attributes, would it be easy or difficult?

Exercise

Take a few moments to jot down the things that you love about yourself. Come up with at least twenty things—more if you can. Go on a real rampage about what you love about yourself. It will be very telling as to the type of relationship you have with yourself.

1.
2.
3.
4.
5.
6.
7.
8.
9.
10.
11.
12.
13.
14.
15.
16.
17.
18.
19.

20.
21.
22.
23.
24.
25.
26.
27.
28.
29.
30.
31.
32.
33.
34.
35.
36.
37.
38.
39.
40.
41.
42.
43.
44.
45.

Once you complete your list of the positive aspects of yourself, describe how it felt to do this exercise. Do you have a huge smile on your face? Hopefully so!

Describe your feelings here:

What did you learn from doing this exercise?

If we think we are being modest or humble when we don't know why we are lovable, we are sadly mistaken. What did the greatest man who ever lived have to say on the matter? In Luke 10:27, Jesus said that Christian law included two things: "Thou shalt love the lord … and thy neighbor as thyself." In verse 28, he went on to show the power of applying those two things. He said, "This do, and thou shalt live."

How about that! It does not mean that you are a stuck-up egomaniac when you love yourself. Isn't that cool? In fact, unless we know how to love ourselves, we can never know how to love anyone else. Now, when I learned this principle, it was one of the greatest aha moments of my life. I grew up with the limiting belief that giving too many compliments creates a big ego. Obviously, that is one of those limiting beliefs that I should have questioned decades ago. However, I feel blessed to at least have the privilege of understanding it now. Better late than never, right?

Does Your Face Look Like the Sun?

Exercise

Go to your bathroom mirror, and look straight into your eyes. Force yourself to say these words: "I love, accept, and approve of myself exactly the way that I am."

Make this your practice whenever you are in front of your bathroom mirror. Awkward? Yes, it is, but only for a little while. You will get used to it soon enough. After about a month of saying it over and over, come back and write down what subtle or not-so-subtle changes you notice. So much positive momentum happens when you speak nicely to yourself. You don't let others call you stupid, so why call yourself stupid? You don't let others say you are fat, so why do you call yourself fat? Your brain is a supercomputer, processing everything you put into it. In other words, "Garbage in means garbage out!"

Stop talking trash about yourself, and you'll have fewer trashy experiences to talk about.

Exercise

What did you notice after thirty days of saying that positive affirmation?

_____

_____

_____

_____

Exercise

When you lavish love upon yourself, so as to more efficiently lavish love upon others, how does that look and feel? How does it affect your decisions and relations with other people?

Answer these questions. If I truly love myself ...

- How much sleep will I get?
- Where will I live?
- What will I do with my life?
- What will my friends be like?
- How important will spirituality be to me?
- Will I exercise? If so, how often and by doing what?
- How will I care for my body?
- How will I care for my mind?
- How will I spend free time?
- What will my attitude be toward needs versus luxuries?
- Will my home and car be in good repair?
- Will I live in clean, uncluttered surroundings?
- Will I smoke, abuse alcohol, or take drugs?
- Will I have a habit of holding grudges or resenting others?
- How long will it take to forgive an offense against me?

If you are thinking that this idea of saying "I love, accept, and approve of myself" makes it sound like you think you're perfect just how you are and that there is no room for improvement, that is not the case. If God can love us as mere imperfect dust, why can't we love ourselves? Aren't we to follow his example? That's not even considering what happens if you try saying the opposite: "I hate myself, and I don't approve of myself at all." Isn't that truly motivating? I bet you can hardly wipe the smile off your face. Make sense now? Just try it.

Ideas for Lavishing Love upon Yourself

- Wake up slowly, taking time to get into a positive mind-set before your feet hit the floor.
- Include some stretches in your day.
- Get outdoors and stop to smell the roses, acknowledging all the beauty in nature.
- Get a massage—ninety minutes this time.
- Get a facial.
- Instead of doing your own nails, this time go and have them done professionally while you meditate or enjoy reading a great book.
- Buy a cashmere sweater.
- Stay open to making nourishing, new connections with stimulating people.
- Drink delicious wine.
- Dine in style, even if you're at home. Why not use a tablecloth, light some candles, and play some soft music in the background?
- Buy fresh flowers for your home.
- Eat great food.
- Forgive everyone.
- Love everyone.
- Stop being critical and judgmental.
- Learn what your own body loves, and let it have what it needs to think.
- Laugh as much as possible.
- Dance in the rain.
- Go on vacation (especially if you'll have a butler and pillow menu).
- Have an attitude of gratitude.
- Drink water, lots of it.

- Oil your skin from head to toe.
- Learn about vitamins, supplements, and essential oils.
- Eat fewer genetically modified organisms.
- Wear a fragrance that uplifts you.
- Read.
- Run.
- Go to a movie that uplifts the spirit.
- Learn to be comfortable in your skin.
- Be still.
- Be generous with your hospitality.
- Honor your father and your mother.
- Show love toward your family.
- Exercise the fruits of the spirit.
- Be nicer than is necessary.

Try This On for Size

Go to your bathroom and light all of your scented candles. Place them around your tub. Turn on the water to a temperature you love. Add a hydrating bubble bath, a few drops of lavender and lemon oil, and either a cup of olive oil or a cup of coconut oil.

Next, head to the kitchen and grab a martini shaker.

DN Martini

Ingredients:
2 shots of vodka
1 shot of lime juice
1 shot of orange liqueur
1 ½ shots of orange juice, pomegranate/blueberry juice, or cranberry juice

Does Your Face Look Like the Sun?

Instructions:
- Place ingredients in shaker. Shake vigorously.
- Dip the rim of a martini glass in water and then in sugar.
- Pour the contents from the martini shaker into the sugar-rimmed martini glass.

Head back to your bubbly, oil-infused, perfumed bath, which should be just about ready. Pull the covers back on your bed so that you can fall right into it after your bath. Lay out your sleeping clothes so that's all taken care of.

Play your favorite music softly as you step into the bubbly, essential-oil bath. Place a rolled towel behind your neck and your DN martini at your side. Feel the stress melting away as the music fills the air. Now your body is feeling totally relaxed, the cocktail is delighting your taste buds, and the aromas and fragrances are delicious in the air around you. Is this what you would call lavishing yourself with love? Just add rose petals!

Exercise

Follow the above steps exactly. Soak for a minimum of twenty minutes, and pay attention to all five of your body's senses. Write down what you noticed after this bath in comparison to what you normally notice after a quick, rushed shower.

Observations:

Chapter 8
How Well Are We Nourished?

Typically, when we speak of being nourished, we are referring to food, although we may include things like vitamins, minerals, and supplements. How often do we really think of being nourished in a much grander sense? Nourishment has to do with what sustains our lives. This includes foods, but it also includes anything that promotes our growth and wellness and helps us to improve and feel balanced. When we stop to consider the grander scope of being nourished, it seems that we should take a look at the other things that can affect our support, growth, and sustenance.

Would you agree that our relationships can be included in the consideration of how well nourished we are? In some cases, people may even be suffering from malnutrition because of some of their relationships. Earlier, we discussed whether or not it served us in a positive way to participate in the economic crisis of 2007–2008.

Perhaps we should question the relationships we have chosen to closely participate in. We need to love—*period!* However, do we need to spend a lot of time, energy, and focus on the relationships that do not cause us to feel nourished? Think about it.

Exercise

Write down your ten most nourishing relationships.
1.
2.
3.
4.
5.
6.
7.
8.
9.
10.

Does Your Face Look Like the Sun?

Now go back and review your list of your ten closest friends.

1.
2.
3.
4.
5.
6.
7.
8.
9.
10.

Does the list match? If not, why not?

Analyze the ways in which you feel nourished or sustained by your ten most nourishing relationships.

Let's try to expand these types of relationships. Clearly, it adds momentum to our journey to learn love of self.

Chapter 9
What Is a Soul Mate?

Webster's dictionary defines a soul mate as someone who understands and connects with you in every way and at every level, which gives you a sense of place. It is one you feel great resonance with.

Writer Richard Bach said, "A soul mate is someone who has locks that fit our keys, and keys to fit our locks. When we feel safe enough to open the locks, our truest selves step out, and we can be completely and honestly who we are" (Richard Bach, *The Bridge Across Forever. A Lovestory. New York: Dell, 1986, 388*).

Does Your Face Look Like the Sun?

How cool is it to connect with people who can make us feel like no pieces of our puzzles are missing?

Here is a list of ten elements of a soul mate relationship:
- The feeling is unexplainable. It is a deeply ingrained and recurring feeling that no words can express.
- A soul mate gives you a sense of nostalgia. It will feel as if you have known each other your entire lives even though only a short period of time may have passed.
- You're on the same page. Without using words, you can look at each other and know what the other is saying.
- You love the person completely. You love your soul mate for the good qualities he or she possesses and are more than willing to put up with any imperfections.
- It is an impassioned experience. The level of intensity can be higher than that of other relationships in good and bad situations.
- You are a team. No matter what life throws at one or the other, you know it will be okay because your soul mate will be right there with you. Your relationship is endowed with spirituality, love, and peace.
- You are mentally in sync. Like twins, you and your soul mate connect and are aware of that connection. You may be thinking of each other at the same time, or you might just know when something is wrong with the other even when you're apart.
- Your soul mate makes you feel content. Whenever you are with this person, you feel that everything's going to be okay and that no harm could possibly happen. He or she always builds you up.
- Life without your soul mate is unfathomable. It is not a relationship that you can allow yourself to just give up on. You know that every relationship requires work, and you are more than willing to put that work in.
- When you speak, you never take your eyes off of your soul mate. You are speaking directly to him or her. Your attention cannot be easily swayed because of the deep connection you share.

Having the experience of a soul mate—or better yet, several people who mate with your soul—is truly a treasure. It will create more joy, laughter, and fun than you can ever imagine.

Exercise

How many relationships do you feel truly mate with your soul?

Exercise

What qualities from the list of elements of a soul mate relationship can be found in your list of soul mates?

Exercise

What new discoveries did you make while analyzing the meaning of *soul mate*?

"I have great hopes that we shall love each other all our lives as much as if we had never married at all." —Lord Byron

"I have learned that to be with those I like is enough." —Walt Whitman

"True friendship is a plant of slow growth, and must undergo and withstand the shocks of adversity before it is entitled to the appellation." —George Washington

Chapter 10
Inspiration

When we think about our faces' looking like the sun, doesn't it make sense that inspired beings have a lot of light or glow to them? Inspiration gives us energy, it motivates us, and it makes us feel excited and happy.

As a hairstylist, I tend to find inspiration in the oddest places. One evening, I was walking around Manhattan, and I saw a horse and carriage. Of course, in the city that never sleeps, all kinds of lights were flickering around me. All of a sudden, I noticed the way the light was reflecting off of the horse's coat. It was striking to me, so I photographed it and took it with me to a class I was attending. There, I used it to create a hair-color placement technique based on the illusion that had happened with the horse.

Now, that may sound pretty far out. Honestly, though, we had been assigned to walk the streets of New York for homework, looking specifically for inspiration that we could share the next morning to create new designs. If I am being totally honest, I am not so sure that the horse would have caught my eye otherwise.

That exercise was powerful for me. It taught me a very valuable life lesson. It gave me pause, causing me to examine what beauty and details we miss out on while walking around in a fog. As a result, I wanted to increase my awareness and heighten my consciousness in order to enjoy more of the beauty and the good happening around me. Boy, does that change your perspective and increase positivity!

When you are more of a deliberate creator of your life experiences and you are engineering your days rather than just letting your days happen to you, the difference is hard to put into words. When I decided to plan this four-part series titled, "Does Your Face Look like the Sun?" a ton of time and research was required. It seems so crazy to me that, after doing all of that work so that the event would be successful, I feel that nobody benefited from it more than I did.

When you stand before a crowd and your desire is to captivate your audience, you must feel really confident about what you are sharing. Knowing that I was not learning just to learn but was learning to teach, I had to be very purposeful in my preparations.

Becoming familiar with so many new things and so many new ways of using our minds was blowing my own mind. It made it so much easier to try to inspire others when I felt inspired and excited by what I was going to share. I was practically bursting with enthusiasm because I had already begun practicing some of these ideas and techniques. My days were shifting because my attitude shifted once I learned how to influence my emotions. I learned that it is up to me to determine what types of thoughts I choose to let linger in my mind and for how long I allow those thoughts to stay.

Paying attention to how my body feels was such a great experience. Now, if I feel sluggish, I don't just push through and ignore it. I question it. My body cannot be feeling sluggish for no reason. I ask myself what I ate, how much sleep I got, and how much water I drank. It's part of my routine now.

We are not typically taught to question why we feel how we feel. So often I hear statements like, "Oh, yeah, all the people in my family get diabetes," "I suffer from migraine headaches," or "I have diverticulitis," "irritable bowel syndrome," or even "psoriasis." Life is not that random. There is no way someone out there is saying, "Eenie, meenie, miney, mo … zap! I think I'll give that family cancer, this family diabetes, this family stomach ulcers."

Yes, it is counterintuitive in this part of the world to question why, but that does not mean that we should not ask anyway. What would happen if we began to ask why we were experiencing a symptom instead of just ignoring the why and masking the symptom with a drug?

How do we know that we couldn't get rid of that symptom if we knew why it happened in the first place? Pay attention to what you did right before the symptom manifested. The next time you get a stomachache, ask yourself things like, **Where was I? What did I eat? How much did I eat? What or how much did I drink?** Remember that garbage in leads to garbage out.

There is no way to have our bodies cooperate with us if we don't give them a reason to. A lady came into my salon with a giant coffee cup in her hand. When I asked her about the coffee allergy I knew she had, she simply shrugged her shoulders and said, "Oh, yeah, I know, but I need this to wake up, so I'll just suffer for it later." Anyone who knows me can already picture the expression on my face. Sadly, though, this is the kind of remark I hear from people every single day.

My daughter figured out that if she eats anything with MSG or nitrates, she will suffer from a debilitating migraine headache. Some can be so bad that she cries and vomits. Do you picture my daughter waking up after the pain subsides and being eager to eat Chinese food or beef jerky? No way! Whenever this first began happening to her, I would ask her what she ate. It was very easy for her as a young girl to make the connection. Rather than eating the Chinese food and popping pills, she has chosen not to eat the food. If she really wants it, we have found ways to get it without the MSG and nitrates.

It would be ludicrous on her part to eat what does not serve her well and then complain about how sick she feels. We can all take more responsibility for how we feel and how well we function by questioning. Even if we choose to take medication for any discomfort we may experience, we must admit that we are not deficient of that medication. We may be deficient of a vitamin, a mineral, a fluid, or something that naturally makes up our body cells, but drugs have not ever been part of our body cells.

We live in an information age. If we want to know the types of things that could contribute to certain symptoms, we search for information about them on the Internet. Not only will we see all the things that we could have done to get sick, but we can see what types of natural products are available to reverse those symptoms.

Health food stores and the produce aisle at the grocery store are my favorite places to feel good. There, we find things that are already in our cells. That is why we won't suffer side effects from them like those that can result from drugs. For everything that a drug can help, there is something natural that will help, too.

Have you ever heard someone say, "I drank eight glasses of water yesterday, I had my green juice, I took my vitamins, and I got thirty minutes of cardio in, and I woke up sicker than a dog"? Not likely. You may, however, have heard something like, "Man, all I ate yesterday was pizza and donuts, and all I drank was beer and coffee, and now I feel like garbage."

Doesn't that sound more like what we hear? It's nuts! Of course, the common solution is to go to the doctor, get a prescription, fill it, pop the pills, and ease the discomfort, only to then suffer from the side effects, which just so happen to be dizziness and nausea.

You probably weren't as sick originally as you became when you started popping pills. A couple of years ago, my sister severely injured her back and ended up with two herniated discs. When she got to the doctor, he prescribed her a medication that was supposed to offer pain relief. Not only did the pain increase, but the possible side effects of the pills were extreme nausea and weight gain.

She did not know what to do because she was in agony. She decided to go ahead and take the prescription medication, hoping and praying that the side effects would not happen to her. Wrong answer! She didn't take them long enough to allow for the weight to pile on. She did, however, get violently nauseated to the point of vomiting.

Have you ever thrown your back out from coughing or sneezing? Have you ever had a pinched nerve or your back out and felt what laughing too hard did to it? Well, just imagine having two herniated discs and a pinched nerve and vomiting. For my sister, that took things to the stratosphere, causing her to be flat on her back for four months. The retching left her unable to walk. Thanks a million, Doc!

Thankfully, my brother-in-law was able to wait on her hand and foot. They found an alternative therapy using a type of traction device. She had to be stretched on it for an hour every day. Taking that pill, with its crazy side effects, let to a bill of twenty thousand dollars to undo the damage.

We are all so grateful to the practitioner she finally found, who is a holistic medical doctor. He does typical Westernized health care but chooses to do things as naturally as possible. It is a great balance. After four months of treatment, my sister was able to walk again and resume working.

After a story like that, I hope someone feels inspired. Start asking why you can't radiate light. If you feel sick, weak, or fragile, question it.

Chapter 11
Do You Love Being Sick?

Do you hear anything? Is that evil little voice in your head causing you to doubt whether this mind-set can help you? Sometimes we have to turn down the volume on the naysaying voices, and sometimes we must simply hang up the phone.

We all know the concept of cause and effect. We understand that for every action, there is a reaction. We also know that for every choice, there is a consequence. Even the Bible tells us that we reap what we sow.

Why would these philosophies apply if they were not also referring to the way our bodies function? Have you ever known anyone with chronic wheezing, sneezing, and congestion? My friend would actually make hacking noises in public like she was coughing up some nasty phlegm. Her husband's ability to ignore it was beyond me. Every time I heard it, I cringed. One day, I noticed that she was making no hacking noises. Finally, I had to ask her why, and she said, "Oh, yeah, I forgot to tell you that I stopped doing dairy products."

Wow! Just like that, one can go from beast to beauty. If you think about it, wasn't cow's milk intended for baby cows? How awkward would it be to see a human being fed by a cow the same way as a baby calf? It is something to consider.

After I was born, my mother did not breast-feed me, for whatever reason. Thank goodness, my four siblings and I had a more enlightened mother where health was concerned. As it turns out, I was severely allergic to dairy products—so much for baby formula. After my digestive system almost completely stopped working, my mother tried goat's milk. I guess things got slightly better, but my body never acted quite right when I was a newborn. It seemed like I would catch every illness, and my allergies were ridiculous. My skin would break out, and I'd wake up with bumps all over or weird patches on my skin. My immune system must have been compromised because, out of five kids, I was the only one who ended up with things like measles and tuberculosis even though we were all exposed to them.

My fascination with asking questions began at a young age because I wanted answers. I had plenty of reasons to be on a search. I wanted to understand how my body worked. Actually, it turned out to be a blessing in disguise that from an early age I began taking responsibility for how my body feels and how it performs.

People often think I am crazy now. As soon as someone says they have to get their child's tonsils or adenoids taken out or to have tubes put into their ears, I start the questioning. Apparently, doctors don't encourage patients to abstain from all dairy products for a month and see if things clear up.

It should not be assumed that people would prefer to change their diets instead of going under the knife. Sadly, the average person views surgery as a quick fix, or instant gratification. People would rather lose body parts than make adjustments in their lifestyles and keep their parts.

Don't you love hearing, "Oh, I am just going to have my gallbladder taken out. I don't need it anyway"? If our tonsils, adenoids, appendixes, uteruses, kidneys, lungs, or other parts were not needed, then why did God put them there in the first place? Just because we can live without a certain body part or organ doesn't mean we should be quick to get rid of it. Personally, I like the idea of sticking with the original design. Tampering with the Creator's work doesn't sound like a good idea to me.

How much differently would we do things if we knew we had only one chance to get it right? What would you do if you knew you needed both lungs to survive? Would you still smoke? How about our kidneys? Would we work harder to learn what keeps our kidneys functioning properly so that we could keep both of them? Gallstones in the gallbladder are typically caused by a diet high in saturated fat. If we couldn't live without a healthy, functioning gallbladder, how much deep-fried goodness would we ingest?

Haven't we all heard, "Move it or lose it"? Why is it, then, that some people are so afraid to get moving? Is it because of the fear that they might sweat or get winded? People will even put seats in their showers. This is for real! A completely able lady let me use her bathroom once, and I actually saw a seat in her shower. There were also needles laying around, apparently for injecting insulin. I also saw candy wrappers, empty bags of chips, and a bowl of pasta surrounding her as she sat on her couch. She literally sat all day long. Why? Why? Why?

Some people must really love being sick. They must! What other possible explanation could there be for such ludicrous decision making? Do you know how hard it was to see that and not scream, "What is wrong with you? Are you trying to kill yourself?" Talk about setting yourself up to fail.

There is no way in the world that she thought the pasta and chips qualified as low-carb fare. That stuff turns into sugar almost as fast as sugar turns into sugar. Her poor little pancreas.

As I plug in and pay attention to the conversations people have with each other, I notice something. Being sick is a real attention getter. Think about it. The sicker you are, the more sympathy you will get. People will make soup for you when you have a cold. You can even get someone to hold your hair back for you while you throw up. People will listen to you and pay attention to you and even wait on you hand and foot. Why get better and stay better? You will lose out on all of that loving attention. Nobody will be there to say, "Aww, you poor baby. I am so sorry. Can I rub your feet for you?"

When was the last time someone volunteered to rub your feet when you were healthy (unless it was a nail tech at a great salon and you happened to be getting a pedicure)? It was probably the last time you told someone that you were sicker than a dog and that a foot rub would make it better, right? Tell the truth.

Do you want to know what my mom did when we got sick? You'll never guess. She completely ignored us. She said people who are babied when they get sick will find ways to stay sick even longer. At the time, it seemed like cruel and unusual punishment. Now, it makes sense to me. Being sick has never been anything I've viewed as glamorous. As far as getting attention goes, I do not want someone seeing or hearing me blowing my nose, hacking, sneezing, wheezing, sweating, or throwing up.

There are too many productive ways in the world that will get me attention if I actually want it. If I want a foot rub, a back rub, or any other kind of rub, I will call a massage therapist, a reflexologist, or even one of my kids in a pinch.

The next time you start whining about how sick you are, pause. Think about your motive. Is it because someone asked you why you are green, gray, or beet red? In that case, it is understandable. Perhaps we have a habit of letting our imaginations run away with us as soon as we find someone willing to listen. We just start babbling on to the poor, innocent victims about every bump, bruise, tension knot, pain, itch, scratch, sprain—you get the point. Pay attention. Have you ever heard of the power of suggestion? When I was a young girl, my sister and I had to go to the doctor for yet another throat infection. One day, the doctor must have been sick of it because he lowered the boom. He looked at the two of us and said, "If you two get one more throat infection, I am taking your tonsils out."

Let me assure you of something. Even though we were young, he did not have to say it twice. Our eyes immediately became the size of saucers. It was clear that we both had the exact same thoughts going on in our heads—*He is not getting my tonsils!*

You may think I am making this stuff up; I am not. My sister and I decided that day never to get another throat infection, and we never did. It must be DNA because most people do not think this way. In fact, I would venture to guess that many people would have said, "Obviously I'm going to get another throat infection, so we might as well just book the surgery."

Admit it. You know you hear people saying things like that on a regular basis. More people need to beware of self-fulfilling prophecies. Talk about "hung by the tongue."

While attending a seminar in Chicago with friends, a man sitting behind us kept coughing. Actually, I am putting it very mildly. He sounded like he was leaning forward to get even closer to us when he had to cough. It was that nasty, thick, phlegmy kind of cough. We kept thinking a chunk of mess was going to come flying out of his mouth and land straight on our necks!

During the lunch break, my friend asked me what I thought about our phlegm-filled friend. I laughed and told her I was wondering if she was wigging out too, but she said she was worried about his making us sick. Actually, I wasn't worried about getting sick as much as I was thoroughly grossed out and appalled by his horrendous manners. The funniest comment came from a lady sitting across the table who overheard our conversation. She said, "Oh, no. Now that you mention it, there was someone seated near me that was coughing too. Shoot, I actually feel a fever coming on ... 'cause, you know, I've got lupus!"

Yes, I realize that it is rude to laugh at ridiculous people, but I couldn't help myself. I literally burst into a fit of giggles like a silly little girl. How could I possibly help it? Need I even say that she may qualify as someone who not only loves being sick but that she might actually be in love with being sick? It just works for some people.

Exercise

In the following space, write down all of your ailments, discomforts, and diseases.

1.
2.
3.
4.
5.
6.
7.
8.
9.
10.

Yes, I am allowing you only ten distresses. Feel better? Good. Now you are free to stay off the distressing topics. Let them go! I promise you that once you begin to distract your focus from being ill, you'll forget you ever were. Doesn't that sound exciting?

Home Remedies

Following are some of my favorite home remedies, passed down through the generations.

Fever
- Place either pure lemon or peppermint oil on the bottom of your feet. It must be medical-grade essential oil. My favorite brands are Young Living, Imani, and Doterra. Remember that you don't need to fret about a low-grade fever. A fever indicates that your body is fighting on your behalf. The heat is needed to kill infection.

- Tip: Children prefer the lemon oil because the peppermint oil can make them feel cold.
- Either oil is great for fever. You can also diffuse it in the room of the person with the fever.
- If skin is not sensitive, place drops of oil down the spine and gently rub it in. If skin is sensitive, dilute the lemon or peppermint oil with almond oil.

Insomnia
- Diffuse medical-grade lavender oil in your bedroom. You can rub it on the bottom of your feet, as well.
- Tip: Be sure that you have a bedroom that is peaceful. It would not be wise to have a television or blaring music on. Keep the room cooler and dark at night. Make sure your mattress and bedding are comfortable. Clear any clutter out of your room. Too bright of a wall color could be a stimulant for some people. A soak in a hot bath with a few drops of lavender while you sip hot chamomile tea and listen to soft classical music can be a nice way to prepare your brain for sleep.

Best Oral Health and a Brighter Smile
- Brush teeth once or twice a week with baking soda and peroxide. Put a drop of medical-grade clove essential oil on your toothbrush before you brush. (It's hot!)
- My favorite brand of natural toothpaste is Tom's. The company makes its own natural mouthwash, as well.
- If you want a great way to remove bacteria, place 1 tablespoon of organic raw coconut oil in your mouth and swish for 20 seconds prior to brushing. This is called an oil pull. Do not swallow any of the oil; spit it out. You will have pulled bacteria out, so you won't want to ingest it.
- Don't forget to floss.

Dry, Flaky Skin

- Combine raw sugar with olive oil in a bowl with a few drops of lavender oil. Step into a warm shower and begin scrubbing, using a circular motion on your skin from head to toe. If you have any calluses on the heels or balls of your feet, you may want to use a pumice stone there.
- Do not use soap on your skin to remove the sugar; simply rinse it off.
- To remove excess moisture, gently pat the skin dry.
- Next, hydrate skin with pure organic raw coconut oil. It will melt with the heat of your body. Massage it in gently from head to toe and enjoy your glow.

Joint Pain

- The greatest remedy I have found for joint pain and sore muscles is to reduce inflammation in the body.
- Taking greens into your body twice a day will automatically decrease swelling around the joints, which decreases discomfort. My favorite brands for greens are It Greens by It Works and also Juice Plus. Use whatever high-quality greens you prefer.
- The other thing I find to be hugely impactful is removing sugar, dairy products, flour, and any nightshade foods from the diet. Nightshade foods include potatoes, tomatoes, peppers, and eggplants.. These can cause flare-ups, so avoid them.

Ear Infection

- Heat helps control pain. Place a heating pad or hot water bottle against the ear. You can also use a warm cloth or rice-filled heating pad. Make sure it is cool enough not to burn the skin.
- Alternatively, you can bake an onion for 20 minutes with the skin on. Slice it in half and let it cool until it won't burn the skin. Hold it cut-side down against your ear until it is no longer warm. It helps to clean infection from the ear.
- Tip: If anything is coming out of the ear, like pus, do not put anything inside the ear. It will heal.

- Place a drop of medical-grade lavender oil behind the ear. This helps clear infection and relieve pain. Rub oil gently down behind the ear and along the eustachian tube (the curve around the ear, behind the jaw).
- Garlic and mullein oil is highly effective in healing faster. Most health food stores sell it ready-made.
  - If you must make it yourself, you will need four to five cloves of garlic, crushed or minced. Let them sit in a saucepan for 15 minutes (this allows the oxygen to activate healing properties).
  - Next, add ¼ cup dried mullein.
  - Add 1 ounce of olive oil, coconut oil, or a combination of oils.
  - Place the saucepan inside of a larger saucepan half-filled with water, or use a double boiler. Turn on heat and warm the oil, but do not allow the garlic to cook. Once the oil is warm, turn off the heat and let it sit. The hot water in the pan will keep the oil warm for quite a while.
  - Once oil reaches body temperature, strain out the garlic and herbs. Use a coffee filter to remove any solids.
  - Optional: You may choose to add 1 drop of tea tree oil, 1 drop of eucalyptus, 1 drop of lavender, and 1 drop of oregano. If skin is sensitive, this may be too strong. This mixture can speed up the healing process but is not required.
  - Store the oil in a glass jar. Do not use until the temperature is comfortable on the inside of your wrist.
  - Use a dropper to put 2 or 3 drops into the ear. If any pus comes out, though, don't put anything inside the ear canal.
  - Use once an hour until clear.
  - Apply some of the oil to the bottom of the feet and cover feet with socks. This will speed up the effectiveness of clearing the infection.
  - If the ear drum is perforated, oil can be applied behind the ear once an hour and to the bottoms of the feet every 3–4 hours.
  - If the ear has produced pus, I would recommend putting a baked onion against the ear because the ear drum is

perforated and contact will be more indirect. You may place a few drops of the garlic ear oil on a cotton ball and tape it over the ear opening.
- If you're able to get it down, swallow some finely chopped garlic mixed with a spoonful of raw honey. This mixture, even in small amounts, is very potent and helps kill infection.
- Keep the ear elevated. Stay propped up because lying flat increases pressure and pain in the ear.
- A high fever will make a child tired and inactive. If the child becomes limp, cannot focus on you, or is in any way unresponsive, immediately seek medical attention. High fevers cause dehydration, so have the child drink a lot of fluid. A good choice is coconut water because it has a ton of electrolytes.
- *Disclaimer:* I am not a doctor. Feel free to consult whatever medical or naturopathic doctor you feel comfortable with. As I stated in the beginning, these are some of my personal favorite remedies for my family. We prefer to do things as naturally as possible in our family. You must do what you are comfortable with. By using natural remedies like these, my family has been able to avoid taking any antibiotics or having any drastic medical procedures.

Bronchitis

- Suck on natural lozenges or menthol drops to numb the back of the throat, diminishing the urge to cough.
- Hot tea with raw honey has antibacterial and anti-inflammatory properties. Use herbal tea like chamomile for its calming properties.
- Use steam to clear the sinus airways and help eliminate mucus. You can steam in a hot shower; or you can pour boiling water into a bowl, place a towel over your head, and put your face over the bowl, breathing in the steam. Do not make contact with the water.
- Use a humidifier in the house to moisten nasal passages so they don't get cracked and painful.

- Stay hydrated with water and tea to dilute mucus and reduce postnasal drip in the back of the throat.
- Clear the air. A cough can be aggravated by the air in your home. Air out the house to purify the air, cleaning out scents from scented sprays, cleaning products, perfumes, and cigarette smoke.
- Use a nasal spray to shrink swollen nasal tissues so sinuses open up.
- Instead of a cough suppressant, try a hot toddy. Combine raw organic honey, lemon, and whiskey with hot water and sip.

If symptoms persist with a fever for longer than two weeks, you may want to seek medical advice or treatment.

Tip: When you feel cold symptoms coming on, immediately increase the amount of immune system support. Vitamin C crystals in orange or grapefruit juice work wonders. Taking more herbal immune-system boosters is also helpful. Apple cider vinegar (raw and organic) can help speed up the healing process.

Constipation
- Drink tons of water.
- Eat tons of leafy greens that have a high water content.
- Take a digestive enzyme with meals.
- Eat prunes, or combine these ingredients into a drink:
  - ½ cup prune juice
  - 1 tablespoon lemon juice
  - 1 cup water
- Get outside and get moving with the goal of breaking a sweat.

"Sometimes all we need to get things moving is to get ourselves moving." —Donaylle Nicole

Itchy, Dry Scalp and Brittle Hair That Breaks Off or Never Seems to Grow

- Massage aloe vera into the scalp. Leave for an hour, and then rinse with warm water.
- You can also rub any of these into your hair:
  - Grape seed oil
  - Coconut oil
  - Jamaican black castor oil
  - Coconut milk
  - Jojoba oil
  - Shea butter
- Shampoo only as necessary.
- Detangle using your fingers instead of a comb.
- Cool-rinsing product oil helps to support strength because the top layer of the hair will be tighter, not allowing so many free radicals to attack the integrity of the hair.
- Schedule a keratin protein treatment. Keratin is what hair and nails are made of, and the keratin treatment is like wrapping hair around hair, thus increasing strength and elasticity.

Upset Stomach

- Drink hot peppermint tea. You can also place a drop of peppermint oil on the tongue.
- Ginger tea with raw honey is nice if there is any nausea associated with the upset stomach.
- If you notice stomach discomfort only when you eat, you may need a digestive aid with meals. Some essential oils are effective with digestion. A good one is Young Living DiGize Oil. Even one drop on your tongue can help with indigestion.
- For menstrual cramps, I have found nothing to be as effective as a hot bath or a hot water bottle or heating pad against my abdomen.

Bladder Infection
- Cranberry and blueberry juice are good for preventing further bacterial growth.
- Papaya fruit has diuretic properties, which increases the amount of urination and speeds up the elimination of bacteria.
- Asparagus, spinach, cashews, and almonds contain sulfur and are effective for clearing up the infection.
- Mix 1 teaspoon of olive oil and 1 teaspoon of garlic juice with one cup of warm water. Consume 3 times daily before meals.
- Another drink that kills infections is 1 teaspoon of raw organic honey and 2 teaspoons of organic apple cider vinegar in 1 cup of water.
- During a bladder or a urinary tract infection, drink plenty of water to flush out bacteria.
- Personally, I prefer taking cranberry pills over the juice because, that way, I do not need to ingest sugar while trying to heal.
- Avoid tea, coffee, chocolate, spicy foods, tomatoes, cheese, alcohol, scented soaps, powders, perfume, and tight underwear.
- Stay very clean to stop the spread of bacteria.
- Your local health food store can recommend other supplements specifically designed for a healthy bladder and urinary tract.
- Press a hot water bottle or heating pad on the lower abdomen for pain relief.

Elevated Blood Pressure
- Garlic can be used to lower hypertension and cholesterol
- Eat more potassium-rich vegetables and low-glycemic fruits like avocado, celery, broccoli, cauliflower, onion, cabbage, lettuce, tomatoes, and berries. Try to get in 4–6 cups per day to improve results.
- Reduce inflammation by changing fats. Instead of butter, margarine, or other saturated fats, replace with coconut oil, olive oil, or organic ghee.
- Lower your intake of sugar and grains.

- Reduce caffeine, which increases stress levels due to the insulin spike.
- Switch from table salt to sea salt, which contains minerals.
- Use a lot of fresh herbs in meals.
- Eat wild fatty fish like wild pink salmon and sardines. These reduce the risk of cardiovascular disease.
- Eat foods containing magnesium, such as pumpkin seeds, spinach, halibut, Swiss chard, sunflower seeds, summer squash, turnip greens, seaweed, and tomatoes. Magnesium increases blood flow and lessens constriction related to hypertension. Magnesium supplements also help.
- Avoid alcohol, which can increase free radicals.
- Put 3–4 cups of Epsom salt into the bathtub daily to lower stress and increase detoxification pathways in the body.
- Drink 8 cups of filtered water with lemon at least once every day. Dehydration causes blood vessels to constrict, resulting in more strain on the heart.
- Get moving. The body was designed to move. Find ways to increase your movement throughout the day. Maybe wearing a pedometer would be motivating.
- Be sure your doctor is aware of your blood pressure so that he or she can offer guidance and monitor you.

Weak or Brittle Nails

- Copper increases collagen and elastin, increasing cell regeneration. Seafood, kale, and mushrooms are all rich in copper.
- Keep nails and cuticles hydrated with oil or lotion.
- Manganese is great for collagen formation. Foods rich in manganese are spinach, beans, oats, and brown rice.
- Olive fruit extract is a potent antioxidant and anti-inflammatory agent that is great for hair, skin, and nails.
- Take biotin supplements.
- Do not file the nails in a see-saw motion. Go in one direction only when shaping.

- Try not to use polish remover more than once per week.
- Steer clear of alcohol-based hand sanitizer. Wash instead with moisturizing soap.
- Do not let nails grow too long.
- Shape your nails into a "squoval" shape, square with rounded edges. Being too pointed or too oval causes them to be weaker.
- Instead of cutting cuticles, which can create an environment for bacteria to grow, moisturize cuticles and push them back with an orangewood stick.
- Some people need a periodic break from nail polish due to the rate of nail growth.

Hair Loss (Alopecia)
- Coconut oil massaged into the scalp and left for a minimum of twenty minutes or aloe massaged into the scalp stimulates healthy hair growth.
- Grape seed oil massaged into the scalp every night promotes growth.
- Onion and garlic are powerful antifungal and antibacterial properties. Mix them in a food processor, creating a paste. Apply to the scalp to not only prevent hair loss but also stimulate faster and healthier hair growth.
- Arnica oil stimulates hair growth by increasing blood circulation in the scalp and also provides essential hair-healthy nutrients. Massage your scalp with arnica oil.
- Apple cider vinegar stimulates healthy growth of hair and removes dandruff or flakes from a dry scalp. Massage vinegar into the scalp for fifteen minutes prior to shampooing. For optimum results, you can also drink 2 teaspoons in water twice a day.
- Also try mixing 3/4 teaspoon of jojoba oil with 3/4 teaspoon of rosemary essential oil. Rub this thoroughly into the scalp two to three hours before shampooing. Cover the head with a shower cap to increase effectiveness.
- Taking a biotin supplement helps support the health and strength of hair, skin, and nails.

Scarring or Bruising
- Arnica oil reduces the swelling, discoloration, and discomfort of bruising.
- Vitamin C will help strengthen capillaries, making you less prone to getting bruises.
- Aloe vera regenerates cells and works well to help heal bruising or scarring.
- Ice keeps bruises from spreading because it constricts the blood vessels.
- Coconut oil, baobab oil, castor oil, and lavender oil all work to clear up scarring.
- To a 6-ounce bottle of extra-virgin coconut oil, add 6 drops each of helichrysum, frankincense, and lavender. Also add 6 vitamin E capsules. Mix and apply 2–3 times a day.

Stress less
- Dance it out.
- Go for a walk.
- Talk about it.
- Breathe.
- Go to bed earlier.
- Focus on what you can control.
- Reminisce about good times.
- Ask for a hug.
- Look for opportunities in life's challenges.
- Smile.

Tips to reduce Stress
- Every day, do something you really enjoy.
- Get up fifteen minutes earlier in the morning and focus on your breathing.
- Prepare for the morning the night before.
- Don't rely on memory; write it down.

- Don't procrastinate. Whatever you want to do tomorrow, strive to get it done today.
- Set up backup plans just in case.
- Say no to extra projects.
- Get enough rest and sleep.
- Organize your home and work space.

Clearly, I could go on and on, but if I don't stop sharing what I have learned about natural health remedies, I will never finish this book! Obviously, this is the tip of the iceberg. For now, let's try these remedies to see how we like them. Once again, I must remind you that I am not a doctor or any other kind of health care specialist. Rather, I am a passionate stylist who is very solution-oriented!

Learning how the body thrives and excels is something that has intrigued me for many, many years. The more I learn, the more I find that I want to learn. I may in fact be obsessed with this whole process! The difference between me and most others is that I am also obsessed with sharing whatever I learn with others if I think it will help someone. My claim is not to be some health expert. My claim is to love people, love myself, and love my family and friends enough to want us all to prosper. My wish is that we all will have access to the information we need to feel light, happy, abundant, useful, positive, spiritual, hopeful, grateful, and on and on.

My desire is always to share what has worked for me with whomever is interested. You don't have to listen, believe, or experiment with any of it. I just want you to know why I mostly feel good and am usually happy, hopeful, positive, playful, energetic, and healthy. This is a purposeful way of letting life happen to me when I have the ability to influence how my life plays out, and it makes sense to me. Why focus on what I cannot control? I must focus on what I can control or influence.

CHAPTER 12
WATER WORKS

This may sound a bit dramatic, but I feel that the beauty of water in our lives should be discussed. After all, isn't the majority of the body made up of this lovely substance that we usually don't take the time to fully appreciate?

Let's begin by focusing on the emotional and psychological effects that water has on people. It may seem, by the title of this book, that I could potentially be obsessed with the sun. Here's the deal, though: how in the world could anybody love and appreciate the sun without knowing that the opposite is nearby? Could I possibly love the sun without, at the very least, equal appreciation of what balances its greatness? When have you ever been excited to go to the beach, lie by the pool, work in the yard, or take a walk in the desert without knowing that water was waiting for you whenever you needed it?

It is so interesting to me when I contemplate the way that the average person in this country talks about water. How often do you hear somebody say that their favorite beverage is water? It almost never is. That shouldn't be the case!

Have you ever watched the television show *Survivor*? The contestants all want nothing more than food, water, shelter, and clothing. That's it, and at the end of each day during this brutal challenge, no one complains about how badly they miss sodas or wine coolers. It would be crazy if these people suffering in the elements were to ask for a vodka and tonic. They know better. It is in these types of circumstances that we see people in the Western part of the world actually paying attention to how their bodies feel and what their bodies need—perhaps for the first time ever.

The contestants are trying to win one million dollars. That is why they're fully present. They are finally really inspired to pay attention to the bodies that they live inside. Have you ever seen a contestant say that they needed a Twinkie or a Big Mac or a beer to feel on their game and at their peak to perform in a challenge? The fluid that they choose is water. Water! We hear them talking about the right balance of proteins and carbs and fluids. The foods that they seek are fish, plants, rice, and fruit from the trees around them. A chicken is worth more than a bar of gold.

Think about your typical routine. Do you ask yourself about all of the things you have to accomplish in order to customize your diet and drinks for the day?

How often do you hear people talk about the great deals on the ninety-nine-cent fast-food restaurant menus? People love knowing that they can feed a family of five for only ten bucks. Just go through the drive-through and order a cheeseburger, fries, and water for each member of the family. Sorry, I forgot to include tax. For only ten dollars plus tax, five people can have full bellies or at least not go to bed hungry like so many others in this world. Here is my struggle. The other day, I was working late, and I had to attend an important meeting at seven o'clock. My time was running out, and my mind raced back and forth. *Should I eat something quickly before my meeting so I can have time to digest it before I go to bed,* I thought, *or should I wait until afterward?*

Within thirty minutes, the fast-food chicken sandwich that I ended up choosing was beginning to take hold of my insides. My body is used to a lot of good food, green juices, supplements, and meals made from scratch, so all of a sudden, making it to the meeting on time was not the issue. Now the issue was how fast I could get to my car, drive home, and reach the nearest toilet. My body had pushed the reject button, and I almost didn't make it home in time. Was it even worth it? The funny thing is that I had ordered the cheap fast-food chicken sandwich with a bottle of purified water. What difference did that make when I overrode the clean water with fast, cheap food?

Think of food as you think of a woman. Who would ever brag about enjoying a cheap, fast, easy woman? Nobody! So why are we so enamored with cheap, fast, easy food? That sounds ludicrous when we start to really think about it.

Thank heavens for the bottle of purified water that I ordered or I might have been in a real pickle (if you know what I mean).

What do you notice when you drink a lot of water?

What do you notice happens when you need more water?

What determinations are you going to make about your commitment to drinking more water, and why?

Following are my favorite reasons for drinking more water.
- I need water to function properly because every cell in my body is composed of water, including my brain.
- Drinking plenty of water contributes to a cleaner complexion and a more youthful appearance.
- Water increases energy and relieves fatigue. It even aids with focus because our brains are mostly water. Concentration and alertness are boosted by water.
- Water promotes healthy weight because it removes the by-products of fat, reduces hunger, and raises your metabolism. Plus, it has zero calories!

Does Your Face Look Like the Sun?

- Water flushes out toxins through sweat and urination, which also reduces the risk of kidney stones and urinary tract infections.
- It hydrates skin, softens it, and creates more of a glow. It gets rid of wrinkles. Water is the best antiaging remedy around.
- It keeps us regular. It aids in the digestion of our food, preventing constipation.
- It boosts the immune system. A water guzzler is less likely to be sickly. Plenty of water helps fight all sorts of ailments.
- Water prevents cramping and straining. It lubricates joints and muscles so they're more elastic.
- Water puts us in a better mood. It costs us little or nothing, unlike mood-stabilizing or mood-enhancing prescriptions.

Here are a few more reasons I love water:
- The way it contributes to the face's looking like the sun
- The way it keeps things clean
- The way it hydrates the body
- The way it refreshes
- The way it supports life
- The way it soothes and relaxes us during a bath, shower, sit by the pool, scuba dive, snorkel, or a wade in the ocean
- The way it feels in a cool shower and in a drink of water after we have worked so hard and are tired, sweaty, and parched
- The way the earth looks after April showers, which bring May flowers
- The way the skin is made more plump and supple when filled with this wonderful beverage
- The way it cleanses and enhances everything we do

High Water Content Foods
Cucumbers: 96 percent water
Coconut water: 95 percent water
Strawberries: 92 percent water

Watermelon: 92 percent water
Broccoli: 90 percent water
Grapefruit: 90 percent water
Cantaloupe: 89 percent water
Avocado: 81 percent water

High Water Content Healthy Soup

Ingredients:
6 cups water
2 tablespoons vegetable seasoning
1 teaspoon turmeric
1 teaspoon sliced fresh ginger, peeled and cut
2 freshly sliced jalapeno pepper, cut in thin strips
2 cups diced green cabbage
3 sliced carrots
3 celery stalks, sliced
1 cup of green beans
½ cup diced onions
1 teaspoon dried basil
½ cup chopped cilantro

Instructions:
In a large pot, bring water, vegetable seasoning, turmeric, ginger, and jalapeño to a boil. Add cabbage, carrots, celery, green beans, onions, and basil; bring to a boil. Reduce heat and cover; simmer for 20 minutes. Top with cilantro. The vegetables in the soup will remain somewhat crunchy. The spices and seasoning make the soup spicy and flavorful.

Chapter 13
Lavish Love

What could happen to our life experience if we began raising our consciousness to focus on love? Then, if we took that to the next level and focused on lavishing love, what would that look like? How much would our lives be impacted?

That was a very deep concept for me when I was first introduced to it. Deepak Chopra, a very well-known doctor, created a series that suggests that love is an actual art form. The reason that got my attention personally is because I have always felt that when I love, I love hard! Learning that there is a true art to showing feeling and displaying love was very intriguing to me. Christian law says that we must love, so I figured it might be fun to explore different ways of showing a truly *feeling* love.

As mentioned earlier, love always starts within us. If we don't love ourselves, we can't possibly love another in a healthy and productive way. Codependent, obsessed, needy, and desperate love, by the way, does not qualify as healthy and productive love.

The doctor who presented this concept offered some brilliant ideas. He suggested that before doing anything, we should stop and ask ourselves, "Is this a manifestation that I love myself or not?" We need to think about how much that discipline could change our quality of life.

For example, say someone offers you a cigarette. However, you have decided beforehand that you don't simply take what people offer you. Now you check in with yourself to see if it would be an act of love to yourself to take nicotine into your lungs. Furthermore, never again do you simply eat lunch. You pause to see what it feels like your body may need. Accepting the invitation to a dinner party is no longer automatic. Time is such a precious commodity that you really think about whether you should accept that invitation. How will it affect your energy level for what needs to be accomplished tomorrow? How will your presence or lack of presence affect you and the host or hostess who offered you the invitation? Will you be nourished mentally, emotionally, and spiritually, or will you be drained in every way from attending? Do the people invited drink and overeat, causing you to compromise? These are just a few questions that those with a raised consciousness will ask when lavishing love upon themselves comes into the picture.

Do we choose the donut or the veggies with hummus? Do we grab unsweetened ice tea with a natural sugar substitute or a diet soda? Do we choose a dark leafy green salad with balsamic vinegar, lean protein, and a piece of fruit; or a do we go for a cheeseburger, fries, and soda?

Which choices show more evidence of self-love? During a lunch break or any other break at work, how do we spend that time? We have between fifteen minutes and an hour. What do we choose to do with those precious moments? Some people use every spare second to catch up on social media. We may be posting pictures on Pinterest, Instagram, Facebook, or Twitter; instant messaging friends; or checking our e-mail.

What if we went old school? What if we called a loved one and left an encouraging or uplifting message? What if we wrote a handwritten thank-you card or letter rather than sending a thank-you text or email? What if we ate for thirty minutes of our lunch hour and took a walk for the other thirty minutes while listening to uplifting audio recordings or meditating or praying? Which one sounds like it would lavish more love upon ourselves?

Are we in the "black hole"—aka the break room—complaining with the disgruntled employees about where we work? Or do we prefer to be the business cheerleaders, having the back of the company where we work? Which option offers us a better feeling inside? Will gossiping with fellow employees about the boss, manager, and fellow employees uplift us? It is not likely that it will, is it?

Naturally, people who realize that they are created in God's image have an easier time showing and feeling love than not. People are often so miserable because they've chosen not to go with the flow of how we are made. We are made to be happy, joyful, appreciative, loving, energetic, engaged, and interested in all of this great life experience.

If people only realized that every time they are miserable, they are not showing love to themselves because they have lost connection with who they really are. We were all made in God's image. How are we going to be happy in a state of anger, stress, frustration, unhappiness, and hopelessness when "God is love" and we were all made in his image?

God is a happy being. It seems that, if we are made in the image of one who is happy, we had better stop doing the things that will result in our being unhappy. Living a life of unhappiness is simply not natural. That was and will never be what was intended when we came into existence. We were intended to enjoy life.

How on earth can we lavish love upon ourselves with feelings of hatred, disgust, dissatisfaction, displeasure, anger, sadness, despair, hopelessness, pessimism, depression, anxiety, and resentment? Who on earth can find happiness in all of these horrendous unnatural states? You cannot!

Loving ourselves clearly is a must and involves focusing upon getting our emotions into alignment with the one who designed us in love and with love. We must also show appreciation for the gift of life by doing all that we can to correct, align, apply, and feel as much love as possible. It will require focus, though.

Does Your Face Look Like the Sun?

One of the ways that many have found it easier to lavish love is to love with an attitude of gratitude. We must begin tracking and writing lists of positive aspects that result in more and more love being lavished throughout our lives. Once we learn to lavish love upon ourselves in a healthy and productive way, how much more able and capable will we be of lavishing love upon others we love?

Chapter 14
Delightful, Delicate Details

When I wish to lavish love upon those who are my objects of attention, it comes down to the details. One of my hobbies is creating collage art for people. It is kind of like making a dream board or inspiration board. Creating them for others is an artistic medium that has given me a lot of satisfaction.

People are so shocked by the tiniest details revealed in my displays. Some have even accused me of calling parents or spouses to get clues for creating these collages and vision boards for them. They can't believe how I could pick up on their likes, dislikes, and life's passions after just a few times spent together.

It never occurred to me that not everyone is able to do this until the day I brought home what I felt was a thoughtful gift for my husband. He loves baseball, he loves the Detroit Tigers, he loves coffee, and he collects coffee mugs.

Why would it be so strange for me to see a display at Starbucks that included the mug, the coffee, and the Tigers design and immediately know how much he would appreciate having it? It was a coffee mug with the Detroit Tigers logo, including a baseball and a pound of coffee beans.

When I got home and showed it to my husband, he simply stared at me. When I asked why he was giving me a suspicious look, he said he wondered who had told me.

"Who told me what?" I said.

"Oh, don't try to fool me. I know someone told you that I preordered this set."

No one had told me anything. He could not believe that I would know instinctively that he would be pleased with this small gesture.

Never did I think of these small details to be a very big deal. Another day, I was visiting friends who were having a party in Chicago. Whenever I am attending any event that I am invited to, I make it a point to bring a host or hostess gift.

My friend could have knocked me over with a feather. My selections were hair products for fine hair from my hair salon for the wife and a good bottle of local bourbon for her husband. As I handed the gift bag over to the host, I was dumbfounded by his response. He said, "How did you know?"

Of course, I was startled, as I had no idea what he meant. He asked who had told me that he was experiencing hair loss and that his favorite spirit is bourbon. Spooky! I had no idea about either one. In fact, the shampoo system was for his wife, as I had noticed how fine her hair was, and I got the bourbon for him because it was local and came in a super cute bottle.

Yes, I can imagine how silly and shallow this must sound. However, I sincerely had no idea that I was hitting the nail on the head with these gifts. For this reason, I love selecting gifts for people.

Welcoming this challenge is something I get a kick out of. It is really a combination of using intuition and paying attention to the details.

Chapter 15
Quotes to Make Your Face Look like the Sun

"We are not interested in the possibilities of defeat; they do not exist." —Queen Victoria

"Most folks are as happy as they make up their minds to be." —Abraham Lincoln

"Let us tenderly and kindly cherish therefore the means of knowledge. Let us dare to read, think, speak, and write." —Lee Brown

"A person without a sense of humor is like a wagon without springs. It is jolted by every pebble on the road." —Henry Ward Beecher

"Keep your face always toward the sunshine and shadows will fall behind you." —Walt Whitman

"Optimism—the doctrine or belief that everything is beautiful, including what's ugly." —Ambrose Pierce

"I destroy my enemies when I make them my friends." —Abraham Lincoln

"Every great dream begins with a dreamer. Always remember you have within you the strength, the patience, and the passion to reach for the stars to change the world." —Harriet Tubman

"We don't stop playing because we grow old. We grow old because we stop playing." —George Bernard Shaw

"Kindness is a language that deaf people can hear and that blind people can see." —Mark Twain

"I run, but not with uncertainty!" —1 Corinthians 9:26

"The secret of getting ahead is getting started." —Mark Twain

"Act, look, feel successful, conduct yourself accordingly, and you will be amazed at the positive results." —William James

Does Your Face Look Like the Sun?

"All growth depends upon activity. There is no development physically or intellectually without effort, and effort means work." —Calvin Coolidge

"Find ecstasy in life; the mere sense of living is joy enough." —Emily Dickinson

"Happiness is the only good. The time to be happy is now. The place to be happy is here. The way to be happy is to make others so." —Robert Green Ingersoll

"Love of beauty is taste. The creation of beauty is art." —Ralph Waldo Emerson

"Though we travel the world over to find the beautiful, we must carry it with us or we find it not." —Ralph Waldo Emerson

"Without continual growth and progress, such words as *improvement*, *achievement*, and *success* have no meaning." —Benjamin Franklin

"Do not take life too seriously. You will never get out of it alive." —Elbert Hubbard

"Age is a matter of feeling, not of years." —Washington Irving

"The greatest weapon against stress is our ability to choose one thought over another." —William James

"The glow of one warm thought is to me worth more than money." —Thomas Jefferson

"I am determined to be cheerful and happy in whatever situation I may find myself. For I have learned that the greater part of our misery or unhappiness is determined not by our circumstance but by our disposition." —Martha Washington

Chapter 16
Who Are You, Anyway?

If someone came to you and asked you what your life's passion is, what would your answer be? How long would it take you to articulate a clear response? Most people have never questioned themselves about this. Do we know what we are truly passionate about?

One day, this concept hit me right between the eyes. My husband's maternal grandmother is very passionate about natural health, and she decided to host an event on the very topic of passion. Even though I did not understand it, I decided to attend the event in support of his grandma, as well as because of my own love of natural well-being.

As I entered the area where the teacher was explaining the passion test to all of those in attendance, it took only a few seconds for me to realize that the questionnaire wasn't anything I needed to fill out. Knowing my passion has never been hard for me. Until that day at that passion event, I had no idea how hard it can be for others to figure out their life's passion.

Today, I meet people every day who are in college, and very few know what to major in or have decided what they are passionate about. Actually, very few decide what to do for a living based on passion, anyway. Most think about their chances of making a lot of money, giving no thought to how passionate they are about their chosen career paths. How sad.

By the age of five years old, I realized that my life's passion would have to be hairdressing. My mother taught me a three-stranded braid or plait, and I was hooked. Seeing the technique one time was all it took for me to fall in love. Hair and the beauty industry in general became my secular life's passion. My ministry became my spiritual life's passion—but that's another conversation.

When we would visit a shopping mall, I would ask my mom if I could sit in the beauty salons we would pass to watch the stylists at work. I have been in this industry since I was a very young teen, and I still feel the burning passion for it inside.

Does Your Face Look Like the Sun?

Recently, I attended a beauty trade show, and one thing in particular captivated me there. While walking around this huge beauty trade show, I noticed a competition in the corner of the venue. Like any normal person, I wanted to see what could possibly be attracting all of that hyper buzz of excitement.

People were everywhere around that booth. I was too short to see over all the heads, so I was left to peek through the spaces between other human beings. They were not about to give up their spots for a petite female. This was serious business.

What was it? A battle! A battle of barbers from all over Chicago, Illinois. What a spectacle to behold! Male and female barbers from all over Chicago were competing for a grand prize. There were so many barbers that they had to be divided into groups. The competition was broken into three or four rounds so that the judges would be able to accurately do their scoring and so that there was enough space. Honestly, I can't believe how many barbers were squeezed into that small amount of space during each round.

As a DJ played loud, inspiring music, someone on the mike explained every move as all of the barbers performed their craft. No other booth had more energy, excitement, and talent.

Even though I am a hairstylist, I had great respect for these barbers. They ranged from tiny African American female barbers to older women from the Middle East, Mexican men, and African American males in every shape and size. It was awesome! The talent, precision, and artistry were ridiculous. There is no doubt that every man, once barbered with such love and precision, would feel like a million bucks and walk a bit taller afterward.

How nice would it be to know that you had the power to change the way another human being feels about him- or herself? It is work from the outside in that can be as impactful as work from the inside out.

My ministry is where I get to have the greatest impact when working from the inside out is concerned. It's kind of like the principle of fishing. You can give a man a fish, but he will only get to eat once. If you teach him how to fish, he eats for life.

The bottom line is this. If you can impact people at any level, you are helping them to improve their lives. If you make people feel better physically, you help them. If you assist people spiritually, you help them. If you counsel people mentally or emotionally or even physically, you are helping them. If you share some great information that you have been taught with others, you are helping them. Can anyone guess what my life's passion boils down to?

You guessed it! Being in the service of other human beings and making a difference in the lives of my fellow man. Nothing in the world feels better to me. It is special to know that I have the ability to affect another human's quality of life.

It doesn't matter if you are as affected in a positive way by words, thoughts, actions, recipes, exercises, examples, or inspiration—as long as you are impacted. I get to live my passion in life; I get to really experience the joy that comes from being alive. It all comes back to helping others.

Does Your Face Look Like the Sun?

Donaylle Nicole's Passion Test

- Tomorrow can't come fast enough; you can hardly sleep. You are so excited. What will you be doing tomorrow?

  _____
  _____
  _____

- The phone rings, and you check your caller ID to see who it is. When you light up like a Christmas tree, who is calling?

  _____
  _____

- What qualities made you light up inside?

  _____
  _____

- When you decline the call, who is it? _____

- What qualities do they possess that cause you to let it go straight to voicemail?

  _____
  _____

- As a child, what did you see yourself doing to make a living?

  _____
  _____

- If there were no obstacles or naysaying remarks discoursing you, what would you do for a living?

　

- Are you doing what you thought you would do?

　

- If so, how do you feel about it now?

　

- If not, why not?

　

- Are there any obstacles present today keeping you from changing your decision from what you didn't want to do to what you did want and still do want?

　

- What holds you back today (if applicable)?

Does Your Face Look Like the Sun?

- When you told your parents about your dreams as a child, how did they respond?

  _____
  _____

- If you are a female, what was your relationship with your dad like?*

  _____
  _____

  *Studies show that a woman's relationship with her father has much to do with her level of confidence and self-esteem as an adult.

- If you are male, was there a lot of pressure to follow in the footsteps of your father?

  _____
  _____

- What activity or activities would you call your hobbies?

  _____
  _____
  _____

- How do you generally fill your spare time?

  _____
  _____

- If you were going to lavish love on yourself, what would you do?

  _____
  _____
  _____

- If there was no such thing as television, computer, cell phones, tablets, and so on, how would that impact your happiness?

  _____
  _____
  _____

- Without modern technology, how would the course of your life be changed?

  _____
  _____
  _____

- How would your days look, specifically?

  _____
  _____
  _____

- When you meditate on your replies to these questions, are you more able to easily discern your passions in life?

  _____
  _____
  _____

- What are they?

  _____
  _____

Does Your Face Look Like the Sun?

- Did this series of questions help you sort them out?

  _____
  _____
  _____

- Do you feel inspired to do more of what you are truly passionate about?

  _____
  _____
  _____

- How do you think living more of a purposeful life will affect your happiness?*

  _____
  _____
  _____

*Sometimes we live as if life is happening to us. While it is true that time and unforeseen occurrences can affect people, we do have some control over our quality of life. What if we woke up with an attitude of gratitude? What if we decided that we would not let our feet hit the floor in the morning until we disciplined ourselves to have a positive feeling? What if we engineered our days in order to have an increased chance of satisfaction? What if we smiled as a habit every morning simply because we woke up and were grateful for another day of life? What if we refused to watch the news or read a newspaper first thing in the morning? What if we woke up and wrote down a list of positive aspects about everyone and everything we would come across that day? What if? Now that's what I call truly getting our minds right!

Chapter 17
Outside In Works Too

Sometimes I wish that every human on earth could be forced to go to France. It is amazing how my own experience changed my perspective.

Of course, I realize that many French people do not love American people. However, if life lessons can be learned in a certain place, why not go? Actually, there are many places in Europe where lessons regarding living from the outside in are more prevalent than they are in the United States.

Years ago, I read a book called *French Women Don't Get Fat* by Mireille Guiliano. I've read it a few times since then, and I will read it again. Guiliano had so many interesting things to say when comparing the lifestyle of the average French person to that of the average American person. She had spent a year as a foreign exchange student in America, and what an impact that year had on her, especially regarding her personal appearance.

The ways that we Americans eat, drink, groom ourselves, and conduct ourselves in public versus in private are very different from the way the French behave. We could all gain so much perspective if we did a lot more international travel and really watched and spoke with the locals.

Once people know you are genuinely interested in their culture, they are happy to share more of themselves, their language, and their lifestyle. This is a great way to lavish love upon others. Learn to be interested in those unlike yourself. Bias against other humans made by God is such an ugly trait. Squash that stuff, broaden your affections, and everyone benefits.

Is it any surprise that Guiliano, the author of **French Women Don't Get Fat**, did, in fact, get fat after just one year in the United States? It was so bad that when she arrived back home to France, her father greeted her with the words, "Why do you look like a sack of potatoes? What happened to you?" She was devastated, as any teenage girl would be. She had always looked just right when she lived in France. But she was carrying extra pounds, and her parents were looking at her like she was deformed.

It is odd how our appearance creates a block to our glow or zest for life, our moods, our attitudes, and our spirit overall. With this devastated young French teen, it was no exception. She became so overwhelmed with sadness over this unfamiliar set of circumstances that her parents decided that they must do the unthinkable.

As a rule, French people do not generally speak of dieting or exercise regimens with one another, especially in public. It can be thought of as a bit tacky. However, in the United States, it is perfectly normal to do so. But the teenage Guiliano became so down about being trapped in her new skin that she no longer recognized herself, so her mother knew she needed help.

With the French, discretion is of the utmost importance when dealing with such a taboo topic. It turned out they were able to find a physician who specialized in weight loss. Over time, the girl's familiar form began to take shape once again. Eventually, she no longer felt disgust when she saw her reflection in the mirror. She made her way back to feeling good in her skin.

This is just an example of the power of taking care of our outsides in order to feel inspired on the inside. We've all heard that beauty lives within. Of course, this is very true. However, there must be a balance of wanting to care for our outsides so that we are motivated to do the personal development and self-care that cause us to radiate the light that lives within us.

When you go to the supermarket and come face to face with another person, how long does it take you to size them up? About two seconds. No one is suggesting that it is right to make judgments based on another person's appearance, dress, grooming, decorum, and attention to detail, but it simply is what happens. Even our hygiene tells a story about us. If I see another woman in the market aisle who is disheveled with no makeup, uncombed hair, dirty fingernails, wrinkled clothing, a sloppy posture, and a less-than-appealing smell, of course I will make a judgment.

Do you know how rare it would be to see a sight like that in Paris, France? It borders on ludicrous—unless, of course, the person is homeless.

When I went to Paris, I was a very young woman of twenty; however, that trip made quite an impact on me. Now, when I go into the market, people often ask me why I am so dressed up. It's weird—I don't feel dressed up at all. Sometimes my clients will ask me the same question. Sadly, there was a time in my life when I don't think anyone would have asked me that at work. How embarrassing that I could have ever rationalized neglecting my appearance before going to work. After all, I do work in the beauty industry. I had to go to another country to get perspective on how a woman should look and act in public. I especially appreciate that experience because, where I live, it seems that many people expect style to be overly casual. People in my community find it completely normal to wear khaki pants to their own weddings. Many of the gentlemen in my town do not own a business suit or a necktie. The problem with working only on the inner beauty is that it is hardly inspiring or motivating.

When you are going to deep clean your house, how do you appear? Do you look just as dirty and unkempt as the house? Try this on for size. How will you be motivated to make your home beautiful, clean, and orderly when you personally are a hot mess? Every time you go to clean a bathroom mirror, you see your reflection looking back at you. Scary! You don't want to clean the house; you want to run and hide under the covers! Who can blame you? Maybe that's why, day after day, you say you are going to clean the house, yet it remains a mess.

We are not inspired to do anything when we feel like a mess. Subconsciously, we may even feel unworthy of living in clean, orderly, beautiful surroundings. It makes sense to me, anyway. Are you going to be dirty while trying to clean?

Remember how the wives and mothers on the old television shows dressed just to be home all day, take care of kids, or run errands? Think of June Cleaver from **Leave It to Beaver**—how she looked by the time Ward left for work in the morning and how she looked when he got back home in the evening. Of course, there was a bit of exaggeration for effect. However, I can see the benefits of this when I really stop to think about it. I can still remember my grandmother getting ready to go see her doctor or her banker. She got completely dolled up to leave the house. It was taken to another level altogether if she was attending church or going to dinner.

What happened to that? What happened to women celebrating being women? Sadly, I have heard women brag about the fact that they don't care how they look; they don't care about hair, skin, nails, body image, or clothing. In France, you will definitely never hear anything so outrageous.

People in France do not brag about not caring about their appearance. They don't think it is admirable not to groom themselves. Leaving the house sloppy, unkempt, or unclean is unheard of, especially for the females. One of the things that impressed me about French women was their ability to pay attention to detail without looking overdone.

Each woman I passed in the streets of Paris made me want to stare a bit longer than what is considered polite. Working in the beauty industry for so long causes me to really enjoy looking at well-put-together people. It is not necessary for someone to be Hollywood or supermodel beautiful in order for me to have admiration and respect for them. It refreshes me to see the care and flair that French women take when they dress for the day.

Proper decorum is something else that I found to be a pleasure. To observe women who are feminine and men who are masculine gentlemen is a delight. Charm and etiquette are so special to see—self-respect on display. What could possibly be wrong with that?

When I stop to consider my mother and her older sister and the care they took with their appearance, I see that it was truly awesome. My mother did not have to travel to Paris for inspiration on being a well-dressed, well-mannered woman. She learned it from her mother and grandmother. Back then, mothers taught their children proper etiquette and good manners. People raising children today are too often afraid of offending their children so they hold back from sharing proper decorum.

In my business, I am surrounded by women every day. That is when the lack of parental guidance becomes all too clear. Women wearing short skirts can be seen with their legs wide apart because no one has taught them the proper way to sit. Some people have no idea that blowing your nose while another is eating is an example of awful manners. Rolling out of bed and going straight to the store or to work in whatever you slept in has become the norm.

Walking through Paris was such a refreshing change. Not only was the women's hair styled perfectly, but it seemed as if the style was created just to flatter them, no matter what current trends dictated. Makeup was applied tastefully, and fragrance was never forgotten; nails were clean and perfectly manicured but never artificial. Skin had a glow, as if a regular facial was just part of being a woman who properly cares for herself. It gave me pause. I felt very inspired walking the streets of Paris and people-watching.

It has been many years since I visited Paris. When I think back to that vacation, the most inspiring part wasn't having lunch in the Eiffel Tower, the fancy bathroom in my hotel room, or staring at the *Mona Lisa* in the Louvre. French food didn't even hold my attention the way watching French people did. The way they experienced life, celebrated small moments, and moved through space, enjoying everything with such passion, was a true inspiration to me. In France, you get the sense that there is so much appreciation and graciousness for seemingly small things—or at least things that we would typically view as small or insignificant.

It was a great life lesson for me. Watching people live with so much gratitude and beauty gave me a lot to think about. For one thing, I definitely learned the value of living not only from the inside out but also from the outside in.

Chapter 18
Move It or Lose It!

Recently, I attended a six-day course that required a lot of sitting. I listened to lectures, participated in workshops, watched video demonstrations, and even listened to some dramatic readings. None of these things involved moving. Each night, after class was over for the day, hours upon hours of homework had to be completed in preparation for the next day of class. Again, no movement was taking place.

Explain to me why, after about day four, I began to experience pain and stiffness. One of the ladies in my class was staying at my home for that week along with her husband. One day, as we compared aches and pains, she said, "Don't you have a hot tub at your house?"

"Goodness, yes!" How could I have forgotten that? Needless to say, that night we sat in that hot tub for a couple of hours, trying to untie all the knots that had been forming. All that sitting had caused more pain than a session with Jillian Michaels. Isn't that crazy? Who knew that being immobile could actually immobilize us?

In recent years, I have not had a gym membership or attended any workout classes like I did in years past. Here is what I have come to discover: for me, personally, movement is movement. My lifestyle requires so much natural movement that I haven't noticed much of a difference between when I was taking Zumba lessons and now, when I am home dancing around with my children or going about my daily routine.

When I went house shopping for my last two houses, something that was important to me was lots of stairs. Most people want to avoid having to climb a lot of stairs, but being forced to climb the stairs is great for keeping the legs strong and even for short bursts of a cardiovascular workout.

Because my bicycle has just a few gears, I have to use more of my own energy to make it go. Parking farther away from my destination just makes sense to me. If I don't have a gym membership, why not create the opportunity for extra movement wherever I am? Think about it. Shouldn't I take the stairs instead of the elevator or escalator if there is time? Why not choose to move it so I don't lose it?

Sometimes I think about how life used to be, about all of the natural movement that occurred not too long ago. People had to move in order to survive. Living on and running a farm was a common way of life. Cows had to be milked; horses had to be groomed and ridden; and eggs had to be collected from chickens. Cages had to be cleaned, as well as barns. Everyone seemed to grow their own food. Some, of course, were more into it than others, but even if a family only grew vegetables, that garden required maintenance. They had to create the space to grow the food, and weeding was a never-ending project. For the colder months, they also had to can vegetables.

Growing up in the country created a lot of movement opportunities for us as kids. My parents did not drive us to the bus stop or to school. We walked to our bus stop and back home again. That alone was a half mile of walking, or running if we were late. Try to imagine any of us neighborhood kids wearing a pedometer in order to track our movements for the day. We grew up on five acres of land. Just going down the hill or to the creek to find wild strawberries was a workout. We didn't know it at the time. Climbing trees and playing tag and pretending we were gymnasts were also workouts. The interesting thing is that we simply thought we were playing or living life. Who knew that we were actually getting exercise?

Let's compare that with kids now, including my own at times. There are days when I tell my children to go outside and play, and they think that means they are being punished. I have to hear things like, "What did I do? I've been good. Why do I have to go outside?"

Trying to imagine the look on my face or my mind-set during these ridiculous exchanges is probably not hard. My mom used to kick us out of the house in the morning and say that we couldn't come back in unless she called us. She used that as a technique not only to keep the house clean but also to keep herself sane. Not having five kids underfoot had to do much for a mother's sanity.

Looking back on it, I am trying to recall exactly when childhood obesity began to surface regularly. As a young child, I'm not sure I ever saw an obese child. It wasn't like everyone was a health nut or doing organized sports. Kids were just kids—chasing one another, playing tag, racing, climbing, biking, falling down and getting back up, sweating, pushing, pulling, wrestling, and so on. That was just life. That's what it meant to be a child. Way back when, people even made up games like Kick the Can, so there was no fancy, expensive equipment needed. All you needed was a willingness to play.

It seemed like having to be more creative with what we did for fun added more to our experience. Before the Slip 'N Slide came out, we made our own. Before remote-control cars and trucks were available, we built our own out of cardboard boxes, and they were powered by our legs and feet. When friends came over, it was common to create dance routines and pretend we were the next trendy girl group to come on the scene. We could dance and sing for hours.

What do kids now do for fun? They go out to eat; play video games; watch reality TV shows; go to the movies; text; tweet; communicate over Facebook, Instagram, Snapchat, and e-mail; and engage in other not-so-mobile or -healthy endeavors. Is it any wonder what has happened to the waistline of the average American youngster? It would have been unheard of thirty years ago or fewer for a teenager to have cellulite, a muffin top, or stretch marks. Girls didn't even start puberty as early as they do now, which causes an entire host of other issues.

Before I completely go off on a rampage of disgust, let's get back to movement. Consider New York City, where people commonly walk everywhere. New York has some of the finest dining establishments in the country. Why is it, then, that if we visit there and stay for an entire week, eating all of the delights we can hold, we don't typically gain weight? After New York–style pizza, lunch at the Turkish deli, French cuisine for dinner, snacks at the street vendors, soul food at Sylvia's in Harlem, drinks at the garage in Greenwich Village, we still experience no weight gain at all?

Now that is the power of movement. When I walk the streets of Manhattan, everyone is moving so fast. People don't seem to need a gym class or a CrossFit membership. It seems like just living in a place that requires constant movement is keeping the people slim, trim, and healthy. When you live in New York City or behave like a native, the amount of movement you engage in and the speed with which you do it is unbelievable. Sometimes you feel that you can't walk another step and decide to hail a taxi, but it's to no avail. You feel like you're going to cry because your legs and feet are so tired. And you're carrying so many packages that you may as well have just reserved a spot in a BodyPump class.

If we are busy moms, work crazy hours, or are on a limited budget, why not find other ways to stay in shape? We are not talking Olympian stuff here. We are talking a regular girl or guy who wants to maintain a normal, healthy weight; increase vitality; have energy; and feel healthy.

Instead of taking the parking spot right next to the store, why not take the parking spot farthest away from the door? Rather than taking the elevator, take the stairs. Don't buy the ranch-style house; buy the multilevel house with tons of stairs and a large yard that requires maintenance. Remember, though, the key is to maintain it yourself, not hire it out. When the kids are dancing around the house, why not join them? You might even teach them a thing or two!

Every time we pass a person with a cane, crutches, or a wheelchair, we should pause. We should always take a moment to be thankful that our arms and legs still work. We need to do what we can and show our appreciation for the gift of mobility. Sitting in a chair is something almost anyone can do. Walking, running, dancing, and climbing are not things everyone can do. What I do know is how people who can't walk, run, or climb must feel about seeing those who *can* do all those things sitting around whining and complaining. Run for those who can't. Walk for those wishing they could. Climb for those with that longing. Be grateful for your ability to move. Realize that the only pain worse than moving a lot is not moving at all. Ouch! Come on, people—let's move it before we lose it!

Chapter 19
Vibrant Living

When I sit and meditate on the things that remind me of the word *vibrancy*, or being vibrant, many things come to my mind. First and foremost, I do think of the sun. It is a hot ball of radiant, reflective energy.

How cool would it be if we could actually feel inspired to remind ourselves and others of that wonderful ball of light? Of course, the sun comes up, and the sun goes down. One thing that we know for sure, though, is that once it goes down for a short time, it will always come back.

Imagine if we chose a life of staying down and never coming back up. How would we affect those around us if they knew that once they were in our presence, they would only have darkness to look forward to? How would we feel if we were to find out that when we arrive, people feel like all the lights just went off in the room? Wow! That's quite a sobering thought!

If that isn't motivation to live an inspired life, I do not know what is. When we are sitting out by the ocean, lounging by a pool with a great book, or taking a lovely hike on a sunny day, what happens when we suddenly notice the sun moving behind a cloud? As soon as we see that darkness beginning to fade, we know what that means. Who just sits there and waits to get pelted by raindrops? Nobody does! We all gather up our things and run for cover before the rain starts.

Do we want to be the kind of individuals that people describe in the same manner? When we walk into a room, does everyone run for cover so as not to be pelted with depressing energy and negative thinking and speech? Really, stop and think about that. The sun comes up every day and then goes down again. The cool thing is, though, that most of the time when the sun goes down, we are getting ready to go to sleep—or at least we should be. That's why people who work overnight shifts so often suffer from dark moods, deeper levels of depression, or codependency. They barely ever get to see the sun and soak up the vitamin D and other mood-enhancing gifts that the sun offers us free of charge.

What a shame to be robbed of this complimentary gift from our Creator! How much harder would it be to live vibrantly if we never actually saw the light? Light is inspiring and motivating. When the sun goes down, we automatically go into a different mode. It is more of a chill mode.

When it's dark, people want to get into their sweat suits or pajamas. They snuggle up for a movie or a great book in the evening. They light the fireplace or have a bonfire in order to get a bit more of the vibrancy they enjoyed when the sun was still up. Clearly, most people slow down more in the evening time. It's a natural thing.

When we are healthy, this should be a chance to recharge our batteries so that when the sun comes back up, we can once again live in imitation of that sun. We want to have energy. We want to radiate light. We want to share our vibrancy with those around us, offering them warmth, comfort, and inspiration. We want to be wanted by others so that our presence isn't like turning out the lights on everyone around us. We want to feel red-hot passion for the things that we do, the life we were given, and the friends and family who touch our lives closely. We want to know when to shine brightest, when to shine softly, and when, like the sun, to go down altogether.

When I was younger, I didn't know the difference between being realistic and being negative. If I went on and on about all that was horrible, I said I was just being a realist. Boy, am I glad I got wind of another type of mind-set! Being a pessimist really wasn't for me. It goes against my nature to believe that nothing is possible and that life is meant to stink every day. It almost makes me shudder to think of how many people consider this normal thinking. Of course, people suffer many atrocities. To try to live vibrantly doesn't mean not acknowledging that life can be very hard and cause distress.

What I am referring to is making the choice to dwell upon the things that are going right more often than what is going wrong. How much does it serve us in a positive way when we talk at length about our distress? Not at all.

Have you ever been around a person who was so negative and depressed that you felt like you were going to vomit? There have been a few times in my life where I was trapped in a vehicle with someone like that, and by the time I was able to leave their presence, I was either very nauseated or developing a headache. Now, obviously, that is extreme, but it really can happen.

No one can control how other people behave. Believe it or not, some people like living crazy. The only thing we can do is monitor ourselves regularly. Taking self-exams in order to know where we are in the vibrancy chart is very important.

We've already discussed the fact that the sun goes up and the sun goes down. Nobody can stay up 100 percent of the time. If we could, then people would begin to wonder what kind of medication we were taking! They may even find it socially inappropriate. For example, if you were attending a good friend's funeral, it would not be an appropriate time to be walking around with a big, cheesy grin. This would be a time to take the edge off of how brightly you are shining. It could seem insensitive and even rude to be too happy at such an occasion. You could, however, be a warm source of comfort and hope to those suffering loss, as the sun also does for us. Therein lies the balance as to how we should imitate the sun appropriately.

Does Your Face Look Like the Sun?

If someone comes to you with major enthusiasm and passion about something and you do not match that level of enthusiasm and passion in return, you could seem like a wet blanket to the other person and actually take away some of their light. How much will they want to come to you the next time they have something exciting to share?

As I am writing these thoughts, I am also reflecting on myself and on raising my personal level of consciousness about this. If I am going to inspire someone else to live with vibrancy, then I must feel vibrant myself. If I want to be around positive, high-energy people, then I must be that way as well.

Living a vibrant lifestyle comes from a heart full of love and gratitude. In recent years, I have tried to make it a point to journal about what I have to be appreciative of. It can literally shift your mindset in a positive way to live with an attitude of gratitude. Try it! For the next thirty days, wake up and mentally design your day to be more vibrant. In the evening, before you lie down to sleep for the night, take a few minutes to begin shaping your attitude of gratitude. It will make you feel so much better. Even if you feel like you had kind of a rotten day, once you start digging deeper, you'll realize the day wasn't so bad after all. It all comes down to perspective. We can literally affect our perspective for the better with this attitude of gratitude.

Exercise

Write a brief description of how you usually come home from a long day. What words do you typically use? How do you generally feel? How would your family describe the way you seem when you get home?

After thirty days, return to this page. Write the answers to the same questions. Be sure to interview each of the people living in your household to see what a difference they've noticed in you. Do not tell them in advance what you are going to do unless they ask. It certainly wouldn't hurt if the whole family practiced this discipline. Just imagine it. Instead of one vibrant person living in your home, you would have an entire household of vibrancy! Now, that would be something!

Chapter 20
Attitude of Gratitude

I have heard it said, "Whatever we express gratitude for, that thing expands." What if there is some truth to that? Personally, when I do something nice for someone and they seem genuinely and sincerely thankful, I can't wait to do something nice for them again. Reciprocity isn't even necessary when sincere expressions of gratitude are offered. We can live off of these expressions for quite a long time. Those acknowledgments really make a difference.

Imagine if every morning, before we allowed our feet to hit the floor, we disciplined ourselves to state what we are thankful for. These are called gratitude affirmations. Some even keep a journal of gratitude. Basically, if we wake up thankful for another day of life and another chance to experience the beauty of living, it can really set positive energy flowing as we begin our day. Why not be responsible for engineering our experiences rather than sitting by, waiting for life to just happen to us?

We do not need to treat our lives as yet another opportunity to be victimized. For every action, there is a reaction, and for every choice we make, there is a natural consequence. Since that is true, why not choose to do things in such a way that we bring about a better outcome? If we know that whatever we express appreciation for expands, we should use that information to create a greater life experience. Yes, of course, it's easier to simply complain, be in a negative state of mind, and live a life full of excuses, but why not agree to try something completely new?

Try waking up every day with a much higher consciousness of your level of thanks. Really think about how nice that could look and feel. If the good that we enjoy is continuously growing because we are consistently expressing gratitude, how cool is that? That really shows how much power we do have to influence the quality of our lives.

When I first heard about the power of having an attitude of gratitude, it made me really try harder to raise my consciousness. Plugging in and paying attention has served me well in this area. When I truly became aware of my level of appreciation, I also found myself more aware of the gratitude—or lack thereof—of those around me.

It is quite appalling, I am ashamed to say. Am I ever glad I chose to really pay attention! Self-awareness is the first step toward improving my emotional intelligence. The next step is increasing my understanding of the emotions of those around me. We may not have a lot of control over increasing our IQs, but thankfully we can do much to improve our EI, or emotional intelligence. So many of us would choose better words if we were more aware of what words we were using in our daily conversations.

Have you ever been in a room or a class full of people and deliberately said nothing in order to just listen? You really have to try this; it will affect your perception of reality. People all claim to want the same basic things in life. We all want to be happy, healthy, enjoy a measure of stability and security, and love and be loved. Next time you are standing in a line or any situation where people are having conversations around you, ask yourself if what people usually talk about is in harmony with what they say they want.

Have you noticed how many people who want more income talk about all the things they can't afford? If they're not using that expression, it may be another scarcity-type statement that suggests a life of lack rather than one of abundance. So often I hear expressions like, "I'm so poor," "I'm so broke," or "I wish I could have or do that!"

Does that sound like an expression focused on gratitude? Does it sound congruent with those claiming to want to experience greater abundance? How can expressions of scarcity and abundance exist in the same mouth? It doesn't make sense to me for those opposing views, ideas, thoughts, and feelings to come from the same individual. Just think about how much resistance that could put up when it comes to our being able to realize our desires with greater ease and flow.

What if we all made it our custom to focus on what we have rather than what we do not have? What if every time someone asked us how we were feeling, instead of saying, "Okay" or "Fine," we said, "Amazing," "Fabulous," or even just, "Very well"?

That kind of positive energy is so contagious. Who doesn't want to be with those who are oozing optimism? Optimism is comparable to feel-good hormones. Our bodies can naturally produce greater amounts of serotonin, oxytocin, and dopamine in response to laughter, positive thoughts, feelings, and experiences.

Isn't that cool? We can improve how we feel inside by changing what we think about, talk about, and focus on. With that being the case, what could possibly be the harm in increasing our resolve to have an attitude of gratitude?

If we think about all that we have to be thankful for and all of the good in our lives, it will take so much time away from focusing on lack, scarcity, and negativity. Try it on for size. At least we won't be repelling our friends, family, and loved ones! When was the last time you couldn't wait to hang out with that wet blanket friend who never stops whining, complaining, making excuses, or talking about how sick he or she feels?

When we have an attitude of gratitude and radiate light, energy, and optimism, people are drawn to us. We end up being the reason others are inspired to be more optimistic, happy, loving, and grateful. What do we have to lose? After all, aren't we all trying to have a face that looks like the sun?

Printed in the United States
By Bookmasters